Practice in Daily Life 19

생활 속의 참선수행 시리즈

Trust yourself and the path appears

나를 알면 길이 보여요

나를 알면 길이 보여요

생활 속의 참선수행 시리즈 19 (한영합본)
대행큰스님 법문

발행일 2025년 7월 1판1쇄
영문번역 한마음국제문화원
표지디자인 박수연
편집 한마음국제문화원
발행 한마음출판사
출판등록 384-2000-000010
전화 031-470-3175
팩스 031-470-3209
이메일 onemind@hanmaum.org

ⓒ2025(재)한마음선원
본 출판물은 저작권법에 의하여 보호를 받는 저작물이므로
무단 복제와 무단 전재를 할 수 없습니다.

Trust yourself and the path appears
Practice in Daily Life 19
Dharma Talks by Seon Master Daehaeng

First Edition, First Printing, July 2025
English Translation by Hanmaum International Culture Institute
Edited by Hanmaum International Culture Institute
Cover Design by Su Yeon Park
Published by Hanmaum Publications
www.hanmaumbooks.org

© 2025 Hanmaum Seonwon Foundation
All rights reserved, including the right to reproduce
this work in any form.

Printed in the Republic of Korea

ISBN 978-89-91857-71-1
ISBN 978-89-91857-50-6 (세트)

차례

  8   머리글

10   대행큰스님에 대하여

24   나를 알면 길이 보여요

168   한마음출판사 출간 도서

172   해외에서 출간된 한마음 도서

174   한마음선원 본원 및 국내지원

CONTENTS

9   Foreword

11   About Daehaeng Kun Sunim

25   Trust yourself and the path appears

168 Books by
     Hanmaum Publications

172 Other Books by
     Seon Master Daehaeng

175 Hanmaum Seon Center
     and Overseas Branches

일체제불의 마음

일체제불의 마음은

내 한마음이다

일체제불의 법이

내 한마음의 법이며 생활이다

일체제불의 몸은 일체 중생의 몸이다

일체제불의 자비와 사랑은

일체중생의 자비와 사랑이다

선행하는 것도 악행하는 것도

다 내 한마음에 있다

The Mind of All Buddhas

The mind of every Buddha is my one mind.

The teachings of every Buddha are

the truth of my one mind and daily life.

The body of every Buddha is

the body of each unenlightened being.

The compassion and love of every Buddha

is the compassion and love

of all unenlightened beings.

Doing good or doing bad all depends upon

how I use my one mind.

머리글

대행큰스님이 지난 50여 년 동안 끊임없이 중생들에게 베풀어 주신 수많은 법문이 있었지만, 핵심을 짚어 내는 하나의 단어가 있다면, 그건 아마도 "참나"일 것입니다. 항상 나와 함께 있어서 보지 못하는 내 안의 진짜 나, 그 "참나"를 발견하여 당당하고 싱그럽게 살아가기를 바라는, 중생을 위한 스님의 간절한 바람은 이 한 편의 법문 속에도 여지없이 드러나 있습니다.

누구에게나 내면에는 만물만생을 다 먹여 살리고도 되남는 마음속 한 점의 불씨가 있습니다. 그 영원한 불씨를 찾아 광대무변한 마음법의 이치를 체득하여, 진정한 자유인으로서, 우주의 한 일원으로서 당당히 그 역할을 해나가길 바라는 대행큰스님의 간곡한 뜻이 이 법문을 통해 여러분 모두의 마음에 전해지길 바랍니다.

한마음국제문화원 일동 합장

Foreword

For over fifty years, Daehaeng Kun Sunim gave countless Dharma talks and teachings to beings without number, but if all those talks could be summed up into one word, it would be "true self."

This true essence has always been with us, yet remains unseen. Discover it for yourself, and in doing so, learn to live with courage, dignity, and joy. That all beings should awaken to this true essence was Daehaeng Kun Sunim's deepest wish. When you've tasted the most refreshing spring water imaginable, you naturally want to share it with others.

Within us all is this seed, this spark that feeds and sustains each and every being. Discover this eternal spark and realize its profound and unlimited ability. If you can do this, you'll know what it means to truly be a free person, and you can fulfill the great role that is yours as a member of the whole universe.

With palms together,
The Hanmaum International Culture Institute

대행큰스님에 대하여

　대행큰스님께서는 여러 면에서 매우 보기 드문 선사禪師셨다. 무엇보다 선사라면 당연히 비구 스님을 떠올리는 전통 속에서 여성으로서 선사가 되셨으며, 비구 스님들을 제자로 두었던 유일한 비구니 스님이셨고, 노년층 여성이 주된 신도계층을 이루었던 한국 불교에 젊은 세대의 청장년층 남녀들을 대거 참여하게 만들어 한국불교에 새로운 풍격風格을 일으키는 데 일조한 큰 스승이셨다. 또한 전통 비구니 강원과 비구니 종단에 대한 지속적인 지원을 펼치심으로써 비구니 승단을 발전시키는데 중추적인 역할을 하셨다.

About Daehaeng Kun Sunim

Daehaeng *Kun Sunim*[1] (1927 - 2012) was a rare teacher in Korea: a female *Seon*(Zen)[2] master, a nun whose students also included monks, and a teacher who helped revitalize Korean Buddhism by dramatically increasing the participation of young people and men.

---

1. Sunim / Kun Sunim: Sunim is the respectful title of address for a Buddhist monk or nun in Korea, and Kun Sunim is the title given to outstanding nuns or monks.

2. Seon(禪)(Chan, Zen): Seon describes the unshakeable state where one has firm faith in their inherent foundation, their Buddha-nature, and so returns everything they encounter back to this fundamental mind. It also means letting go of "I," "me," and "mine" throughout one's daily life.

큰스님께서는 어느 누구나 마음수행을 통해 깨달을 수 있음을 강조하시면서 삭발제자와 유발제자를 가리지 않고 법을 구하는 이들에게는 모두 똑같이 가르침을 주셨다.

스님은 1927년 서울에서 태어나 일찍이 9세경에 자성을 밝히셨고 당신이 증득證得하신 바를 완성하기 위해 오랫동안 산중에서 수행하셨다. 훗날, 누더기가 다 된 해진 옷을 걸치고 손에 주어지는 것만을 먹으며 지냈던 그 당시를 회상하며 스님은 의도적으로 고행을 하고자 했던 것이 아니라 당신에게 주어진 환경이 그러했노라고, 또한 근본 불성자리에 일체를 맡기고 그 맡긴 일이 어떻게 작용하는지를 관하는 일에 완전히 몰두하고 있었기에 다른 것에는 신경을 쓸 틈이 없었노라고 말씀하셨다.

그 시절의 체험이 스님의 가르치는 방식을 형성하는 데 깊은 영향을 미쳤다. 스님은 우리가 본래부터 어마어마한 잠재력을, 무궁무진한 에너지와 지혜를 가지고 있는데도 대부분이 그 역량을 알지 못해 끊임없이 많은 고통을 겪으며 살고 있음을 절실히 느끼며 안타까워하셨다. 우리들 각자 안에 존재하는 이 위대한 빛을 명백히 알고 있었

She broke out of traditional models of spiritual practice to teach in such a way that allowed anyone to practice and awaken, making laypeole a particular focus of her efforts. At the same time, she was a major force for the advancement of *Bhikkunis*,[3] heavily supporting traditional nuns' colleges as well as the modern Bhikkuni Council of Korea.

Born in Seoul, Korea, she awakened when she was around eight years old and spent the years that followed learning to put her understanding into practice. For years, she wandered the mountains of Korea, wearing ragged clothes and eating only what was at hand. Later, she explained that she hadn't been pursuing some type of asceticism; rather, she was just completely absorbed

---

3. Bhikkunis: Female sunims who are fully ordained are called Bhikkuni (比丘尼) sunims, while male sunims who are fully ordained are called Bhikku (比丘) sunims. This can also be a polite way of indicating male or female sunims.

기에, 스님은 본래부터 가지고 있는 근본자성自性인 '참나'를 믿고 의지해 살라 가르치셨고, 이 중요한 진리에서 벗어나는 그 어떤 것도 가르치기를 단호히 거부하셨다.

의도한 바는 아니셨지만, 스님은 매일매일의 일상 속에서 누구나 내면에 갖추어 가지고 있는 근본이자 진수眞髓인 참나와 진정으로 통할 수 있게 되었을 때 어떠한 일이 일어나는지를 역력히 보여 주셨다. 사람들은 스님 곁에 있을 때 자신들을 무한히 받아 주고 품어 주는 것만 같은, 말로 형언키 어려운 정밀靜謐한 기운을 느꼈고, 스님이 다른 사람들을 도와줄 때 드러내 보이는 깊은 법력 또한 목도하곤 하였다. 하지만 이 모든 일들은 당신 자신을 돋보이게 하거나 과시하려 했던 게 아니었다. 사실 스님께서는 당신의 법력을 늘 감추려고 하셨다. 마음공부의 목적이 놀라운 능력을 갖게 되는 것이 아님에도 대중들이 그것에만 집착하게 되는 폐단을 우려하셨기 때문이었다.

그렇지만 당신이 하신 모든 일을 통해, 우리가 내면에 있는 근본과 진정으로 하나가 되었을 때 그 능력과 자유로움이 어떤 것인지를 보여주셨다. 스님은 우리 모두가 근본을 통해 연결되어 있으므로 다 통할 수 있고, 그럼으로

in entrusting everything to her fundamental Buddha essence and observing how that affected her life.

Those years profoundly shaped Kun Sunim's later teaching style; she intimately knew the great potential, energy, and wisdom inherent within each of us, and recognized that most of the people she encountered suffered because they didn't realize this about themselves. Seeing clearly the great light in every individual, she taught people to rely upon this inherent foundation, and refused to teach anything that distracted from this most important truth.

Without any particular intention to do so, Daehaeng Kun Sunim demonstrated on a daily basis the freedom and ability that arise when we truly connect with this fundamental essence inherent within us.

The sense of acceptance and connection people felt from being around her, as well as the

써 서로 깊이 이해할 수 있다는 것을 보여 주셨으며, 더 나아가 우리가 근본자리에서 일으키는 한생각이 이 세상에 법이 되어 돌아갈 수 있다는 것도 보여 주셨다.

어떤 의미에서는 이 모든 일이 우리가 만물만생과 정말로 하나가 되었을 때 자연스레 부수적으로 나오는 것이라고 할 수 있다. 상대를 둘로 보거나 방해물로 여기는 마음이 사라졌을 때, 진정으로 모두와 조화롭게 흘러갈 수 있게 되었을 때 이 모든 일이 가능할 수 있게 되는 것이다. 이렇게 되면, 다가오는 상대가 누구든 별개의 존재로 느끼지 않게 된다. 그들이 또 다른 우리 자신들의 모습이기 때문이다. 일체가 둘이 아님을 뼛속 깊이 느끼는 사람이, 어찌 자신 앞에 닥친 인연을 나 몰라라 하고 등져 버릴 수 있겠는가?

스님은 중생들이 가지고 오는 어려운 문제나 상황들을 해결할 수 있도록 도와주셨으며, 이러한 스님의 자비로운 원력은 당신이 도시로 나와 본격적으로 대중들을 가르치기 이전에 이미 한국에서는 전설이 되어 있었다. 1950년대 말경, 치악산 상원사 근처 한 움막에서 수행차 몇 년간 머무르신 적이 있었는데, 그 소문을 듣고 전국에

abilities she manifested, weren't things she was trying to show off. In fact, she usually tried to hide them because people would tend to cling to these, without realizing that chasing after them cannot lead to either freedom or awakening.

Nonetheless, in her very life, in everything she did, she was an example of the true freedom and wisdom that arise from this very basic, fundamental essence that we all have – that we are. She showed that because we are all interconnected, we can deeply understand what's going on with others, and that the intentions we give rise to can manifest and function in the world.

All of these are, in a sense, side effects, things that arise naturally when we are truly one with everyone and everything around us. They happen because we are able to flow in harmony with our world, with no dualistic views or attachments to get in the way. At this point, other beings are not cut off from us; they are another aspect

서 찾아오는 사람들이 끊이질 않았다. 차마 그들의 고통스러운 호소를 내칠 수가 없었던 스님은 일일이 그들의 말에 귀 기울이며 마음을 다해 그들을 도와주셨다. 스님은 자비를 물 마른 웅덩이에서 죽어 가는 물고기를 살리는 방생에 비유하셨다. 집세가 없어 셋집에서 쫓겨난 사람들에게 집을 마련해 주고, 학비가 없어서 학교를 마칠 수 없는 학생들에게 학비를 대주셨지만, 스님의 자비행慈悲行을 아는 사람은 손에 꼽을 정도밖에 되지 않았다.

그러나 문제를 해결해 주면 그때뿐 또 다른 문제가 닥쳐오면 속수무책이 되어 버리고 마는 사람들을 보며, 스님께서는 중생들이 자신의 문제를 스스로 해결하고 윤회輪廻¹의 굴레에서 벗어나 자유인이 될 수 있는 도리를 가르치는 일이 더 시급함을 느끼셨다. 누구나가 다 가지고 있는 '참나', 이 내면의 밝디밝은 진수眞髓를 알게 하여, 자신들이 자유롭게 사는 것은 물론이요, 자신들의 삶이 인연

---

1. 윤회(輪廻): 산스크리트의 삼사라(samsara)를 번역한 말로 쉼 없이 돈다는 생사의 바퀴를 뜻함. 다시 말해, 수레바퀴가 끊임없이 구르는 것과 같이, 중생이 번뇌와 업에 의하여 삼계(三界: 색계, 욕계, 무색계) 육도(六道: 지옥, 아귀, 축생, 아수라, 인간, 천상)라는 생사의 세계를 그치지 않고 돌고도는 현상을 일컬음.

of ourselves. Who, feeling this to their very bones, could turn their back on others?

It was this deep compassion that made her a legend in Korea long before she formally started teaching. She was known for having the spiritual power to help people in all circumstances and with every kind of problem. She compared compassion to freeing a fish from a drying puddle, putting a homeless family into a home, or providing the school fees that would allow a student to finish high school. And when she did things like this, and more, few knew that she was behind it.

Her compassion was also unconditional. She would offer what help she could to individuals and organizations, whether they be Christian or Buddhist, a private organization or governmental. She would help nuns' temples that had no relationship with her temple, Christian organizations that looked after children living on their own, city-run projects to help care for the elderly,

맺은 모든 이에게 축복이 되어 이 한세상을 활달히 살아갈 수 있도록 해야겠다고 다짐하셨다.

마침내 산에서 내려온 스님께서는 1972년 경기도 안양에 한마음선원을 설립하셨다. 이후 40여 년 동안 한마음선원에 주석하시며, 지혜를 원하는 자에게 지혜를, 배고프고 가난한 자에게는 먹을 것과 물질을, 아파하는 자에게는 치유의 방편을 내어 주시는 무한량의 자비를 베푸시며 불법의 진리를 가르쳐 주셨다.

스님은 도움이 필요한 다양한 사회복지 프로그램을 후원하셨고, 6개국에 9개의 국외지원과 국내 15개의 지원을 세우셨다. 또한 스님의 가르침은 영어, 독어, 스페인어, 러시아어, 중국어, 일본어, 불어, 이탈리아어, 베트남어, 체코어, 인도네시아어 등으로 번역 출간되었다. 스님은 2012년 5월 22일 0시, 세납 86세로 입적하셨으며, 법랍 63세셨다.

and much, much more. Yet, even when she provided material support, always there was the deep, unseen aid she offered through this connection we all share.

However, she saw that ultimately, for people to live freely and go forward in the world as a blessing to all around them, they needed to know about this bright essence that is within each of us. To help people discover this for themselves, she founded the first *Hanmaum*[4] Seon Center in 1972. For the next forty years she gave wisdom to those who needed wisdom, food and money to those who were poor and hungry, and compassion to those who were hurting.

---

4. Hanmaum[han-ma-um]: "Han" means one, great, and combined, while "maum" means mind, as well as heart, and together they mean everything combined and connected as one.

What is called Hanmaum is intangible, unseen, and transcends time and space. It has no beginning or end, and is sometimes called our fundamental mind. It also means the mind of all beings and everything in the universe connected and working together as one. In English, we usually translate this as one mind.

본 저서는 대행큰스님의 법문을 한국어와 영어 합본 시리즈로
출간하는 〈생활 속의 참선수행〉 시리즈 제19권으로
1998년 11월 1일 전국 연합 청년법회에서 설하신
내용을 재편집한 것입니다.

This Dharma talk was given by
Daehaeng Kun Sunim on Sunday, November 1, 1998.
This is volume 19 in the ongoing series,
Practice in Daily Life.

Daehaeng Kun Sunim founded nine overseas branches of
Hanmaum Seon Center, and her teachings have been
translated into twelve different languages to date: English,
German, Russian, Chinese, French, Spanish, Indonesian,
Italian, Japanese, Vietnamese, Estonian, and Czech,
in addition to the original Korean.
For more information about these or the overseas centers,
please see the back of this book.

나를 알면 길이 보여요

Trust yourself and the path appears

나를 알면 길이 보여요

다리 꼬부리고 앉은 사람은 펴고 앉아요. 이게 대수롭지 않은 말 같지만 누가 다리 안 아프게 대신해 줄 수는 없으니까 알아서 편하게 앉으세요.

우리가 하는 이 공부는 지금 차원을 넘어서서 마음으로 뛰는 공부이며 실천하는 공부예요.

Trust yourself and the path appears

As you sit here, if your legs start hurting, please straighten them out and sit comfortably. This may seem like a trivial issue, but no one else will take care of your legs, and no one else can keep them from hurting.

This practice of relying upon our *fundamental mind*[5] is the practice of transcending

---

5. Fundamental mind: This refers to our inherent essence, that which we fundamentally are. "Mind," in Mahayana Buddhism, almost never means the brain or intellect. Instead, it refers to the essence, through which we are connected to everything, everywhere. It is intangible, beyond space and time, and has no beginning or end. It is the source of everything, and everyone is endowed with it. "Fundamental mind" is interchangeable with other terms such as "Buddha-nature," "True nature," "True self," and "Foundation."

우리는 보통 모든 것은 마음먹기에 달렸다고 쉽게 말을 하는데 사실 마음으로 쉽게 뛰어넘을 줄은 몰라요.

나는 여러분들에게 재밌는 말은 해줄 수 없어요. 하지만 진실한 말은 해줄 수 있습니다. 지금부터 하는 내 말을 재밌고 진실하게 들으면 참 감사하겠습니다.

많은 가르침들을 보면 일상생활 속에서 항상 공부하라고 그러죠. 와선臥禪이나 입선立禪이나 좌선坐禪이나 행선行禪이나 둘이 아니라고요. 하다 못해 변소에 똥을 누러 가도 참선이라고요.

ourselves. It's the practice of transcending the level we're currently at by working through our fundamental mind to respond to what we're facing and make a positive difference in our daily life. It's easy to say that everything depends on how we use our minds, but in reality, not many people are able to actually use their minds to overcome what they're facing.

My style of speaking isn't particularly exciting or entertaining, but what I can do is tell you about what's deeply true, so please listen carefully and think about how you can apply it to your life.

If you think about various different Buddhist teachings, you'll realize that they're saying that we have to always practice in daily life. They're also saying that sitting meditation, meditation while lying down, and meditation while walking don't exist apart from your life. They teach that even sitting on the toilet and having a bowel movement can be spiritual practice.

맞습니다. 공부하는 데는 요만한 거 하나 빼 놓을 수가 없어요. 왜냐하면 그 모든 것들은 나로부터 시작되기 때문입니다. 내가 생각하고 몸을 움직이고 그렇게 모든 걸 자기가 하는 거예요. 이러한 나를 있게 한 내 근본마음에 모든 걸 일임하라는 겁니다. 그런데 여러분들이 시작부터 그렇게 하기 힘들거든요.

그렇기 때문에 제가 이런 말을 하는 거예요. 단 15분이라도 시간이 있어서 좌선을 할 때는 반드시 '**주인공**![2] 너만이 네가 있다는 것을 증명할 수 있어'라고 하면서, 오직 내 주인공, 내 근본마음을 믿고 모든 걸 거기에 맡겨 놓고 하라고요. 말로 하라는 게 아니라 '너만이 증명해 줄 수 있어!'라고 하면서 모든 걸 일임하라는 거예요. 그것이 바로 곧장 문을 두드리는 소리와 같은 겁니다.

---

2. **주인공**(主人空): 우리 모두 스스로 갖추어 가지고 있는 근본마음으로 일체 만물만생의 근본과 직결된 자리. 나를 존재하게 하고, 나를 움직이게 하며, 내 모든 것을 관장하는 참 주인이므로 주인(主人)이며, 매 순간 쉴 사이 없이 변하고 돌아가 고정된 실체가 없으므로 빌 공(空)자를 써서, 주인공(主人空)이라 함.

Really. There's not a single thing in your life that can't be part of your spiritual practice. You're the one who moves your body and who gives rise to thoughts, so you have the choice to make it all become part of your spiritual practice. You have the choice to entrust everything to this foundation that's your source. But in the beginning, this is probably going to be a bit difficult.

So, whenever you have 15 minutes or so, practice entrusting everything to your *Juingong*,[6] your fundamental mind, with the thought that, "Juingong! You're the one who has to show that you exist." I'm not talking about doing this with

---

6. Juingong(主人空, [Ju-in-gong]): Pronounced "ju-in-gong." "Juin(主人)" means the true doer or the master, and "gong(空)" means empty. Thus, Juingong is our true nature, our true essence, the master within that is always changing and manifesting, with no fixed form or shape.

Daehaeng Sunim has compared Juingong to the root of the tree. Our bodies and consciousness are like the branches and leaves, but it is the root that is the source of the tree, and it is the root that sustains the visible tree.

일상생활을 하면서 겪는 모든 걸 닥치는 대로 주인공에다 놓으세요. '너만이 길을 정돈해서 잘 가게 할 수 있어'라고 하면서 천차만별의 용도에 따라 적합하게 굴려 놓으세요.

그래야 한바다를 만들 수 있고 모두가 **보림**[3]을 할 수 있게 돼요. 빗물, 흙물, 똥물, 핏물, 어느 물 하나, 더럽고 깨끗함의 구분 없이 바다로 흘러 들어갑니다. 그리고 그렇게 바다가 되어 수증기로 올라갔다가 정화가 돼 내려올 때에는 모두 자기 그릇대로 평등하게 먹을 수가 있죠. 우리 공부하는 것도 지금 그렇게 하고 가는 거예요. 그래서 나쁜 거든지 좋은 거든지, 더러운 거든지 깨끗한 거든지 전부 다 내 근본마음에 놓고 가라는 겁니다.

---

3. **보림(保任)**: 견성한 후에도 게으르지 않는 수행을 통하여 일체가 둘 아닌 도리를 체득하는 것을 말함.

words, you have to actually entrust everything to your fundamental mind, "Okay, now take care of this and prove you exist!" It's like going straight to the door and knocking loudly.

Take whatever you face in your daily life, and as it comes up, entrust it to your fundamental mind, Juingong. "Only you can clear the path in front of me, only you can clear away the brush and logs blocking the way!" Take all the different things and situations you experience and return them inwardly like this.

Sometimes, according to the circumstances, you may need to stay focused on raising a particular intention and continuously returning that. If you keep returning things like this, you will be able to become the one ocean and help everything function together nondually.

Rainwater, muddy water, sewer water, bloody water – whatever – it all flows into the ocean and

안 되는 거는 '되게 하는 것도 너야' 하고 놓고 가고, 되는 거는 감사하게 놓으면서 항상 내 근본마음, 내 주인공에 모든 거를 다 놓으세요.

가는 거 잡지 말고,
오는 거 마다하지 말라

모두들 욕심을 끊어라, 번뇌를 끊어라 이렇게 말하지만 난 그러라는 게 아니에요. 욕심을 끊으라는 것도 아니고 끊지 말라는 것도 아닙니다. 가는 거 잡지 말고 내 앞에 오는 거 마다하지 말아라 이런 소리예요. 모든 걸 내 근본마음에 놓으라는 겁니다.

becomes one with it. It evaporates, is purified, and when it comes down again, everyone is able to drink of it and make use of it according to their capacity. This practice of relying upon our fundamental mind works in a similar way. So, no matter what you're experiencing, whether it's good or bad, dirty or clean, entrust all of it to your fundamental mind.

When things go badly, entrust them to your fundamental mind with the thought that, "It's you who can make things go well," and when things are going well, let go of them with gratitude. Entrust everything to your fundamental mind, your Juingong, like this.

Neither clinging to, nor avoiding

People are told to cut off greed and delusions, but that's not what I teach. Cutting off or not cutting off isn't the way to approach these. The

오는 것 마다하지 말라는 말이, 예를 들어, 훔치고 싶다는 생각이 든다고 그냥 도둑질을 하라는 게 아닙니다. 인간으로까지 왔기에 인간으로서 무엇이 옳은 일이고 그른 일인가 정도는 잘 알 겁니다. 그런 거 정도는 구분하고 달리 마음을 낼 수 있어야 합니다. 다시 얘기하자면 오는 거 거절하지 말고 가는 거 잡지 말라는 얘기는 마음의 중도를 말하는 거예요.

가는 걸 억지로 좇아가는 건 욕심이고 오는 거 자꾸 거절을 하는 거는 그걸 해결하는 과정을 거치지 못하기 때문에 결국 자신을 무능하게 만드는 이치가 돼요. 그러니까 오는 거 마다하지도 말고 가는 거 잡지도 마라 그러는 겁니다. 이해가 됩니까?

real way to deal with them is by not clinging to things that are leaving you, and not trying to avoid the things that are coming to you. Take all of it and entrust it all to your fundamental mind.

Let me be clear. When I say don't avoid the things coming to you, this doesn't mean that if the urge to steal something arises, you just follow it. Having evolved to the level of a human being, you know by now what's right and what's wrong. You're capable of evaluating what you're feeling, and can decide that things should go differently. In other words, not refusing the things that come to you, nor clinging to things that leave you, means to remain grounded in your upright center.

To chase after the things leaving you is to fall into greed, and to try to avoid the things coming to you is to deprive yourself of the experience of working through them, and will leave you

그러니까 오는 거를 억지로 마다하지도 말고 가는 걸 억지로 붙잡아다가 내가 뭐를 하려고 그러지도 마세요. 예를 들어, 하다못해 불사하는 데 돈이 없다 하더라도 나는 괴롭게 하고 가지 않아요. 단 하나 있다면 '너만이 할 수 있어' 하는 것뿐이죠.

내가 여러분한테, 일이 닥치면 '너만이 할 수 있어'라고 생각하고 그걸 자기 자신에게 수시로 말하라고 얘기하지만, 사실은 난 그냥 놓아요. '네가 있다면 하고 없다면 그만둬라' 하는 거죠. 허허허. 그렇잖아요? 내 근본, 내 부처가 있다면 할 거고 없다면 못할 거 아니에요. 그렇게 생활하며 살 수 있도록 노력해야 돼요.

weaker and hinder your evolution. This is why I tell you not to refuse the things that are coming to you, nor to cling to things that are leaving. Do you understand?

So, don't try to push away the things that are coming to you, nor keep the things that are leaving, even if it seems like it's for a good purpose. For example, when it's necessary to build a new temple, then even if I don't have enough money, I don't let myself be bothered by it, nor do I bother others about it. The only thing I can do is entrust it to my fundamental mind, "Only you can do this."

I've told you that when something happens to you, remind yourself that, "My foundation can take care of all of this!" And then entrust that situation completely. But for myself, I just let go of everything. "If you exist, then take care of it, if you don't exist, then get lost!" (Laughs.) My

파도가 치면 파도치는 대로, 잔잔하면 잔잔한 대로, 어떠한 일이 닥쳐온다 하더라도 눈 하나 깜짝 안 하고 그냥 자기 근본, 주인공을 믿고 거기다 놓고 갈 수 있다면 그게 최고예요.

왜 그런 줄 아세요? 모든 일체 만물에 불성이 다 있거든요. 저 돌에도 있고, 나무에도 있고, 꽃에도 있고, 어느 거 하나에도 불성이 없는 건 없어요. 그래서 여러분들이 '네가 있다면 하고 네가 없다면 못 하지' 하는 그런 마음으로 정말 내 근본을 완전히 믿어 모든 걸 놓고 가야 진짜 '너만이 할 수 있어'가 되는 거지, 그게 그냥 할 수 있는 것이 아니거든요. 위급할 때는 더더욱 그렇죠.

foundation, my buddha exists, so it'll take care of this. You need to work at living with this kind of attitude.

Whether the waves are pounding on you, or the sea is calm, have faith in your foundation and keep entrusting it with everything that's happening. Keep working at doing this, to the point where you can entrust everything without even blinking an eye. Being able to live like this is beyond anything you can imagine.

Do you know why entrusting like that works? It is because everything and all beings have this foundation, this Buddha-nature. Even the stones and the trees and the flowers have this Buddha-nature. There is nothing that doesn't have Buddha-nature.

So, have faith in this Buddha-nature, and thoroughly entrust everything to it, with the attitude that, "You're here, so you need to take

일체가 하나 되어 응해준다

그렇다면 여러분들이 그렇게 했을 때 어떠한 일이 벌어지느냐? 여러분의 몸 안에 있는 그 생명들이 다 **보살**[4]이 되어 **응신**[5]으로 화해요.

정히 급하고 아주 큰 문제, 예를 들어, 나라의 큰 일이라든가, 세계적으로 무슨 일이 일어나서 지구가 잘못된다거나 하는 문제가 일어났을 때 우리들 모두가 내 근본을 믿고 일체를 거기에 놓고 가면, 만물만생이 근본마음을 통해 하나가 되어 응신으로 화해 줘요.

---

4. 보살(菩薩): 위로는 불법(佛法)을 닦아 깨달음의 지혜를 얻고, 아래로는 중생을 구제하며 그들이 스스로 깨닫도록 도와주는 부처의 화현.

5. 응신(應身): 법신(法身)이 다양한 중생들을 구제하기 위하여 응해주고 둘이 아니게 모습을 나투어 보살행을 하는 것.

care of this!" Then what you entrusted will be transformed. This won't happen without thoroughly letting go. And when it's a true emergency, you may have to work particularly hard at entrusting like this.

Everything responds as one

Do you know what happens when you truly entrust everything to your fundamental mind? All the lives in your body become *bodhisattvas* [7] and respond to the situation.

When some huge, urgent problem occurs – problems that could affect the whole country or even the world – if each of you has firm faith in your fundamental mind and entrusts every-

---

7. Bodhisattva: This usually refers to a person of great spiritual ability who is dedicated to saving those lost in ignorance and suffering. But it also means the nondual energy of our fundamental nature working to help save beings or assisting them in awakening for themselves.

저기 저런 나무 하나도 그냥 있지 않고 하나가 돼 주고 하다못해 죽은 이들의 영혼도 전부 **한마음**[6]으로 응신이 돼 줘요. 이 소리 헛소리로 들리시죠?

예전에 어떤 사람이 몸이 얼마나 아팠던지 마당에 피어 있던 꽃 한 송이에다, 이렇게 아파서 죽겠으니 어떡하면 좋겠냐고 절절히 관하면서 **비대발괄**[7]하며 살려달라고 했대요. 그랬는데 꿈에 꽃으로 장식을 한 아주 예쁜 선녀가 나타나서는 꽃 이파리 하나하나를 떼어서 그 사람에게 붙여 주더래요. 그리고 그 후로 병이 나았대요. 이런 걸 그냥 재미있는 이야기로만 흘려 버리진 마세요.

---

6. **한마음**: '한'이란 광대무변함, 일체가 하나로 합쳐진 것을 뜻하며, 한마음이란 만질 수도 보이지도 않으며, 시공간을 초월하여, 시작도 끝도 없는 근본마음을 말함. 또한, 만물만생의 마음이 삼천대천세계와 서로 연결되어 하나로 돌아가는 것을 의미하기도 함. 다시 말해, 한마음은 우주 전체와 그 속에서 살고 있는 일체 생명들이 근본을 통해 서로 연결되어 그 마음들이 하나로 돌아가는 모든 작용을 포함하고 있음.

7. **비대발괄**: 억울한 사정을 하소연하면서 간절히 청하여 빎.

thing to it, then all lives and things in the world will communicate with each other through this fundamental mind, working together as one to respond to that problem. Do you see those trees over there? Even they become one. Even the spirits of the dead become one and respond to that problem. This sounds hard to believe, doesn't it?

Several years ago, there was a woman who was very sick and in great pain, and, in desperation, she begged a flower in her yard for help.

That night, a heavenly being adorned with flowers appeared in her dream and plucked petals from the flowers and stuck them all over her body. Afterwards, she recovered from her illness. Don't let the implications of this just flow in one ear and out the other!

우리가 전력이 들어오고 나가고 하는 그 흐름을 보지 못한다고 그게 없는 게 아니잖아요. 전등에 불 들어오고 꺼지는 거 보면서 전력이 들어오고 나가는 걸 알지만 우리가 그 움직임을 보지는 못하죠. 근데 보지 못한다고 해서 없는 거라고 그러실 건가요? 그렇지 않잖아요.

보이지 않아도 여러분들은 전력이 있다는 것도 알고 그걸 다방면으로 사용할 줄도 알아요. 배우고 공부해서 다 잘 압니다. 내 근본마음을 활용하고 쓰는 것도 마찬가지예요. 공부하고 배우면 됩니다. 그런데 여러분들은 해 보지도 않고 때때로 '아, 나는 공부를 못해서 못할 거야'라고 지레 생각하는데 그러지 마세요. 누구나가 다 할 수 있어요. 그래서 배워 실천을 해 보라고 알려 주는 겁니다.

Just because you can't see the flow of electricity doesn't mean that it isn't there. You can see the lights turning on and off, and you know that the electricity is coming and going, but you can't see the movement itself. Would you say that it doesn't exist just because you can't see it moving? Of course not.

Even though you can't see it, you all know that electricity exists and you know how to use it in all kinds of ways. You've observed its effects, used it, and now understand it fairly well, right?

Using your fundamental mind is the same. You just pay attention, practice with it, and learn. But some people don't even try to do this much, and then think to themselves, "It didn't work for me. I guess I don't have the ability." Don't think like that! Anyone can do this. That's why I'm telling you how to practice with this and learn how it works.

늠름하게 살아가라

자기 삶을 과감하게 물러서지 않으면서도 늠름하게 이끌고 싶다면 자기가 자기를 못 믿으면 안돼요. 자기를 있게 한 내 근본마음을 믿어야 합니다. 설사 지금 자기 근본마음을 못 믿겠다 하더라도 가만히 생각해 보세요. 당장 죽겠는 일이 닥쳤는데 그냥 있을 겁니까? '한 번 죽지 두 번 죽냐' 하는 마음으로 죽고 사는 거에 두려워 말고 뭐라도 해야죠. 무서워서 물러선다면 그건 육신에 치우쳐서 한 치 앞도 내다보지 못하는 사람들의 행行입니다.

Live without fear

If you want to lead your life boldly and with dignity, without cringing away from things, you must believe in your true self. This true self, this fundamental mind, is what enables you to exist, so this is what you have to rely upon and have faith in. Even if you don't fully believe in your fundamental mind, at least take a moment to think about it. If something incredibly dangerous happened to you right now, would you just sit there and do nothing?

Don't be afraid of dying. Just do your best with what seems necessary. If you step back because of fear, that's the behavior of those who are unable to take even one step forward because they're too focused on their physical body.

예전에 내가 산으로 들로 다닐 때 있었던 일이에요. 며칠을 먹지 못해 너무나 배가 고파서 큰 나무 옆에 쓰러져 정신을 잃었었어요. 그런데 그 나무에서 머리가 하얗게 센 할아버지가 나와서 물을 떠다 주는 거예요. 그걸 먹고 일어났어요. 이게 그냥 꿈일까요? 이 **마음**[8]의 작용이라는 게 보이질 않기 때문에 꿈이라고 치부해 버리는 것뿐이지 사실 이런 식의 마음 작용은 실제로 벌어지는 일이에요.

한번 또 이런 일도 있었어요. 어떤 분이 찾아와서는 무슨 중요한 일을 하는데 많은 사람들의 마음이 좀 모여야 된다는 거예요. 그 사람 마음이 지극했든 아니었든 간에 어쨌든 그 일이 성사돼야만 했었기에 내가 알았다고 대답을 했습니다. 대답을 해놓고 내가 아무것도 하지 않는다면 거짓말이 되는 거죠. 그리고 거짓말의 대가는 반드시 있거든요.

---

8. 마음(心): 단순히 두뇌를 통한 정신활동이나 지성을 일컫는 말이 아니라, 만물만생이 지니고 있으며, 일체 만법을 움직이게 하는 천지의 근본을 뜻함. '안에 있다, 밖에 있다' 혹은 '이거다 저거다'라고 말할 수 없으며 시작과 끝이 없고 사라질 수도 파괴될 수도 없음. 시공을 초월하여 존재함.

This is a story from when I used to wander around the mountains. I hadn't eaten for days and I was so hungry that I collapsed next to a big tree and passed out. A white-haired old man stepped out of the tree and gave me a drink of water. After drinking that, I came to my senses. Was that a dream? When people can't see the workings of mind, they assume things like that were just dreams or hallucinations. However, the unseen workings of our fundamental mind actually do manifest into the world.

Here's another experience I had. Someone came to me with a project that needed a lot of people's support. Even though he'd never made much of an effort at spiritual practice, the issue he spoke of was an important one, so I said I'd help him with it. Having promised to help, I had to deliver, otherwise my words would be a lie. And there's always a price to pay for lying.

어쨌든 그 일이 있고 나서 어느 날 차를 타고 어디를 지나가는데 말이에요, 엄청 많은 묘지가 아파트같이 산자락에 그냥 쫙 있더라고요. 그래서 거기 묘지에 있는 분들을 다 동원했어요. 이런 말을 하면 여러분들은 이해를 못하기 때문에 내가 말을 하기 참 조심스러워요. 하지만 여러분들도 위급할 때는 그렇게 할 수 있으니까 이 말을 하는 겁니다. 만물만생은 자기 근본마음, 주인공을 통해 전부 하나로 연결되어 같이 돌아가니까 자기 근본을 믿고 가면 할 수 있어요.

어쨌든 그분은 일이 잘 성사되었고 그 후 한 번도 찾아오질 않아 어떻게 지내는지 알 수는 없어요. 그런데 이렇게 남을 도와줄 때는 고맙다는 소리를 들으려고 하거나 그 대가로 무엇을 받으려고 하지는 마세요. 그거는 이 공부를 하는 데에 있어서 어긋나는 겁니다. 평소에 내가 어쩔 수 없는 사람을 도와야 할 때에는 도와야 한다는 그 마음 그대로 그냥 해야 합니다. 그렇게 해야 한마음으로 돌아가요.

Some time afterwards, I happened to be driving past a huge cemetery that covered the hills with graves. So, I mobilized all the spirits in that cemetery to help with that project. I'm cautious about saying this, because some of you might think it's too unbelievable, but I'm bringing it up because you, too, can do something like this in an emergency. Because everything and all beings are working together as one through their fundamental mind, Juingong, you can accomplish anything if you are relying upon your fundamental mind.

Anyway, his project went well, but afterwards he never came to see me again, so I don't know how he is doing now. Regardless, when you help someone, don't do it expecting gratitude or some reward. For that goes against the nature of letting go. When you have a sense that you need

당신의 근본마음은
상상 그 이상으로 소중한 보배

내 근본마음이 작용하는 묘하고도 깊은 뜻을 얼마나 알려드려야 여러분들이 알아듣겠는지는 모르지만 이해하지 못하더라도 이걸 우습게 생각하진 마세요. 여러분들의 불성이 수억 겁을 통해서 지금의 여러분들을 형성되게 한 장본인이에요. 진화시켜서 이렇게 여기까지 이끌고 온 장본인이라구요. 얼마나 소중한 보배인지 모르시죠? 꼭 알아야 돼요. 자기가 지금 못났든 잘났든 말이에요.

to help someone, just help them accordingly. This is working together as *one mind*.[8]

Your fundamental mind is a treasure beyond imagining

I keep talking about these profound and mysterious workings of our fundamental mind because these are something that everyone has to understand. But even if some of what I say doesn't make sense to you, please don't take it lightly. This Buddha-nature has led you through eons and has shaped who you are now. You don't realize how much of a precious treasure it is. Regardless of where you're at in life, of how

---

8. One mind(Hanmaum [han-ma-um]): From the Korean, where "one" has a nuance of great and combined, while "mind" is more than intellect and includes "heart" as well. Together, they mean everything combined and connected as one. What is called "one mind" is intangible, unseen, and transcends time and space. It has no beginning or end, and is sometimes called our fundamental mind. It also means the mind of all beings and everything in the universe connected and working together as one.

과거 한 생 한 생 살면서 자기가 어떻게 살았느냐에 따라 모두 주어진 모습이고, 주어진 삶이고, 주어진 어려움입니다. 이런 것을 누구에다 항거抗拒를 합니까? 자기가 몰랐을 때 모르고 잘못한 것이 더 많지 잘한 것이 더 많겠습니까?

그런데 이 마음자리는 자기가 새롭게 입력하면 앞서 입력됐던 것들을 지울 수가 있어요. 그러니 이왕이면 좋은 행을 입력해서 안 좋게 했던 일들을 지우는 게 좋겠죠? 하지만 좋은 일이라고 생각해서 한 것이 의도치 않게 남을 해치는 나쁜 일이 될 수도 있기에 좋은 행을 입력한다는 건 말처럼 되는 게 아닙니다.

smart you are, how old, how poor, or anything else, you truly need to understand this fundamental mind for yourself.

How you've lived each life in the past has set the course for your current life, your situation, your body, and your difficulties. So, can you really resent someone else for how your life turns out? Having lived without knowing your foundation and your connection to the whole, how likely is it that the good things you've done would outweigh the harmful?

The way this fundamental mind works is that when you reinput something, that is recorded over the old version, erasing it. Wouldn't it be nice to go and erase all of the bad things you've done and replace them with good things? However, it's not as easy as that, because what you think of as good or desirable may turn out to be something that eventually harms others.

그러니까 내 근본에 모든 걸 놓고 관하라는 거예요. 다시 말해, 어떻게 해달라, 어떻게 해야겠다 하는 이런 생각을 하라는 게 아니라 모든 걸 다 그냥 내 근본마음에 놓아 한마음으로 돌아가게 하면서 지켜보고, 거기서 뭐가 나오면 나오는 대로 근본마음에 다시 돌려놓는 이 과정을 계속 반복하는 겁니다.

그러다 보면 설사 과거에 살인과 같은 악업이 있었다 하더라도 점차 그게 사라질 거예요. 그러니까 몰라서 저질렀던 **무명**[9]의 업이 없어진다는 얘기죠. 이 **마음공부**[10]라는 것이 참 위대하고 말로는 형용할 수 없는 겁니다.

---

9. **무명**(無明, avidya): 사성제(四聖諦)(고(苦)·집(集)·멸(滅)·도(道))의 진리에 통달하지 못한 마음의 상태로써, 무지(無知), 어리석음, 지혜가 없음을 뜻하며, 이로 인해 진리를 바로 볼 수 없게 되고, 생로병사(生老病死)에서 비롯되는 모든 고통과 번뇌의 근원이 됨.

10. **마음공부**: 진정한 자유인이 되기 위해 자신의 마음이 어떻게 작용하고 변하는지를 관찰하고 배우며, 그것을 실제 생활 속에서 응용하고 체험해 보면서 알아가는 모든 과정을 뜻함.

This is why I tell people to just entrust everything to their fundamental mind. Don't get too caught up in trying to find a particular solution, or in begging for help. Instead, entrust everything unconditionally to your fundamental mind, and then observe what happens. See what comes back out, and entrust that as well.

Keep entrusting and observing like this, over and over, and then what was done in the past, even the karmic effects of murder, will gradually disappear. All the things you did when you were ignorant will melt away. For when you entrust something in this way, it automatically becomes one with your foundation, and in so doing, it transforms into something new and harmonious.

There's just no way I can fully describe the incredible nature of this practice of relying upon

언젠가 내가 스물 몇 살 때였는데 그때도 내가 잘 먹질 못해 길에서 이만한 소똥에다가 머리를 박곤 쓰러진 거예요. 그러니까 그게 소똥이다 뭐다 분간할 힘이 있었다면 그렇게 되지 않았을 텐데 너무 기운이 없다 보니까 넘어져서 일어나지 못하고 있었어요. 그런데 그때 누가 와서 근처 개울에다가 데려다 놓고는 닦아주는 거예요. 그래서 누군가 봤더니 주위엔 전부 갈대숲으로 빽빽했고 그 갈대 속에 큰 나무가 한 그루 서 있더군요.

마음공부 안 하는 사람은 서로 통하지 않아 모르겠지만 이 마음공부 하는 사람은 다 알게 돼 있어요. 그래서 알았어요. 보이진 않았지만 거기에 있던 갈대들과 나무가 나를 씻겨준 거였어요. 물론 사람들이 보기에는 씻어지지를 않았겠지요. 그런데 그들이 다 씻어주니까 내가 정신을 차릴 수 있게 돼서 내가 스스로 물가로 가서 머리에 묻은 똥을 전부 씻어냈죠.

and communicating through your fundamental mind.

Once, when I was in my twenties and didn't have a thing to eat, I was so hungry that I collapsed as I was walking along a country lane, and my head landed in a pile of cow dung. What's worse, I was so weak that I couldn't move my head out of it.

I was barely conscious when someone came and took me to a nearby stream and started to clean me up. But as I began to recover and looked around to see who was helping me, all I saw was a dense thicket of reeds, with a large tree in the middle of it.

Those who don't practice relying upon their fundamental mind probably won't understand what happened, because they don't have the experience of communicating with other lives through their fundamental mind. But those who

어떻게 생각하세요? 이건 내가 씻은 것도 아니고 그쪽에서 씻어준 것도 아닙니다. 왜, 있잖아요, '일체제불의 마음'[11] 노래 말이에요. 거기에 나오는 가사처럼 일체제불의 마음이 만물만생과 더불어 같이 하는 이치를 말하는 거거든요.

다시 말해, 일체제불의 마음은 곧 만물만생의 마음이 둘 아니게 같이 돌아가는 그 한마음이기 때문에 마음들이 어떻게 돌아가는지 그 자리에서는 다 알 수가 있어요. 한마음은 그러한 모든 마음들을 이끌며 진화하도록 하는 겁니다.

---

11. **'일체제불의 마음'**: 대행큰스님이 읊으신 게송에 곡을 붙인 선법가. 게송의 내용은 다음과 같음. "일체제불의 마음은 내 한마음이다. 일체제불의 법이 내 한마음의 법이며 생활이다. 일체제불의 몸은 일체중생의 몸이다. 일체제불의 자비와 사랑은 일체중생의 자비와 사랑이다. 선행하는 것도 악행 하는 것도 다 내 한마음에 있다"

have, will know that it was the reeds and tree that washed me. They washed me and cleaned me up, although to someone else it looked like my head was still covered in cow dung. After a bit, I was able to regain my senses and go to the stream and wash.

Think about this for a moment. This washing wasn't done by myself, nor was it done by something else. You've all heard the song, *"The Mind of All Buddhas,"*[9] right? It speaks of this truth, saying, "The mind of buddhas works together nondually with all beings."

To put it another way, the mind of buddhas is none other than the nondual functioning of the minds of all lives and things, thus this one mind thoroughly understands them and guides them and helps them evolve.

---

9. This song, *The Mind of All Buddhas*, appears at the front of this book.

예를 들어, 착한 목신으로서 자기를 지키고 나갈 수 있는 그런 위치에 있는 나무는 다 응신으로 화해서 자기한테 달려있는 이파리 하나라도 같이 갈 수 있게 그렇게 진화를 시키거든요.

아까도 얘기했듯이 더러운 거든 깨끗한 거든 전부 한바다로 흘러가게 내 모든 것을 다 보림하세요. 그렇게 분별없이, 둘 아니게, 흐르는 그 자리에 하나가 되게 하면 자동적으로 정화가 됩니다. 정화되어 나오는 것들을 용도대로 쓰고 또 그 한자리에 모두 놓아 정화되게 하는 거죠. 이걸 반복하는 거예요.

그러면서 진화되고 능력이 커지면서 더 많이 그 한자리에 놓을 수 있고 거기서 나오는 걸 용도대로 사용하고 먹고 하는 거죠. 만물만생은 근본마음을 통해 서로 연결되어 있기에 나의 이러한 행은 모든 이들에게 도움을 줍니다.

For example, if a tree has been evolving its consciousness in a kindly direction and reached the point where it can protect itself and continue to deepen its development, then it naturally guides even its tiniest leaves forward.

As I mentioned earlier, even after you've experienced your true nature, no matter whether something is dirty or clean, keep letting it go to your fundamental mind so that it can all flow into the one ocean. When you entrust things so completely that they become one with this place and flow nondually, they are automatically purified. Once that happens, they can be used as needed, and when you return what you now experience to this flowing oneness, it is purified all over again.

Then, as you evolve and your ability grows, you can entrust more and more things to this one place. You can make good use out of what comes back out, and what comes back out will

예를 들면, 깨끗이 정화된 물을 먹는 나무들은 크면 큰 대로 작으면 작은 대로 요만한 떡잎까지 자기 생긴 대로 필요한 만큼 먹으면서 자라거든요. 그래서 이렇게 작용하는 전체를 **평등공법**[12]이라고 하는 거죠.

그러니깐 '나는 중생이 돼서 몰라' 이렇게만 하고 주저앉았질 마세요. '나는 더하고 덜함도 없이 용도에 따라서 오는 대로 내가 먹을 것이고, 닥치는 대로 분별없는 그 자리에 놓을 거고, 닥치는 대로 걸을 것이고, 물러서지 않을 것이다'라는 투철한 마음으로 하세요.

---

12. 평등공법(平等空法): 우주 삼라만상 전체가 공체로서 공생, 공용, 공심, 공식하며, 둘 아니게 하나가 되는 이치. 서로 도우면서 함께 작용하는 가운데 균형과 중용이 자연스레 적용이 되며, 끊임없는 변화의 과정 속에서 모두가 고정됨이 없이 찰나찰나 화(化)하여 무수히 나투며 돌아가게 됨.

sustain you. Further, because all life is connected together through this fundamental mind, your spiritual practice will benefit everyone else as well. And then, like when rain falls across the land, the big trees, small trees, and the tiniest sprouting plants will all drink according to their capacity and need.

This one mind of ours works like this. It works like this in every place and time, and for every single being, enabling all of us to grow and evolve.

So, don't just flop down on the ground and say, "I'm only an unenlightened being. What can I do?" Instead, give rise to the firm resolution that, "I'll stay calm and centered regardless of whatever shows up! I'll entrust everything to this one place, my fundamental mind, which is free of all discriminations! I will go forward doing my best, and I'll be utterly relentless about this!"

그렇게 하다 보면 나 자신뿐만 아니라 남들도 건질 수 있게 됩니다. 지나가다 불쌍한 사람이라도 보면 그냥 지나치지 말고 그 사람을 위해 관해 주면 그 사람이 괜찮아질 수 있는 그런 겁니다.

그런데 때로는 그냥 둘 때가 있기도 해요. 너무 모르는 사람은 그래 봤자 정말 아무 소용이 없기 때문에 그 사람 스스로 조금이라도 알게 하기 위해서 내버려두는 수가 있거든요. 내버려 둬도 그 길을 터득하게끔 내버려두는 거지 그냥 내던져 두는 건 아니죠.

아무튼 여러분들도 너그러운 마음, 지혜로운 마음을 가지고 공심共心으로서, 공체共體로서, 공용共用, 공식共食을 하시라 이겁니다.

우리가 산다는 건 일체 만물만생과 다 공생共生하고 있다는 말 아닙니까? 작게 보시면 여러분들의 몸이 공체입니다. 그 몸속에서 수많은 생명들이 공생하고 있어요.

As you learn to live like this, you can save not only yourself, but also others. When you see people having a hard time, don't just ignore them. Instead, raise good intentions for them from this deep place. Then, they'll probably be okay. That said, sometimes, it's better to leave them alone. There's no use trying to help someone who's too caught up in ignorance – you need to leave them alone so that they can learn on their own. This isn't abandoning them, it's letting them learn on their own.

Anyway, what I am telling you to do is to be generous and wise, and to practice giving and receiving, and nourishing each other through your fundamental mind, for we are all connected together as one.

If you think about it, "living" means living and working together with everything and all beings. Look at your body, it's a collection of lives,

내가 내 눈으로 뭘 본다는 건 '나'라는 게 뭐 혼자 따로 있어서 볼 수 있는 게 아니에요. 내 몸 안에 있는 모든 생명들이 다 뒷받침을 해주니까 보는 거죠. 한 군데만 무너져도 그냥 같이 쓰러지게 돼 있어요.

보이지 않는 세계의 일들도
대처할 수 있다

그리고 지금 벌어지는 모든 일들은 현재의 일이지 과거의 일도 미래의 일도 아니니까 과거나 미래에 얽매이지 마세요. 자기가 가는 길을 물러서지 말고 그대로 뚜벅뚜벅 갈 수만 있다면, 다시 말해, 보이지 않는 데서 생기는 일은 보이지 않는 데서 대처해 나가게 하고, 보이는 데서 생기는 일은 당신네들 몸으로, 보이는 육체로 같이 대응해 나가면 힘들더라도 걸림없이 대처해 나갈 수 있을 겁니다.

living and working together as one. There are so many different lives there, all working together, aren't there? When you see something, there isn't a separate "you" seeing "it" over there. You see something because all the lives in your body are working together to make that perception possible. Yet if those lives don't work together, if just one part of your body breaks down, the rest of your body is done for, isn't it?

You can take care of even things that come from the unseen realms

Everything that's going on is happening now, right here – it's not in the past and it's not in the future, so don't get caught up in these. Try to keep going on your path, taking one step after another. If things of the unseen realm arise, entrust them and let the unseen realm deal with them. When it's an issue of the material realm, then also

이 세상에 살면서 일어나는 모든 일이 내 눈에 다 보여 알 수 있으면 얼마나 좋겠습니까? 그런데 그렇지 않거든요. 예를 들어, 악성균 하나가 내 몸에 들어와서 주둔한다면 내 눈에 보이는 것도 아닌데 그거를 어떻게 대처하겠습니까?

그래서 공심共心으로 돌아가는 이치를 알고 공심이 되도록 해야 한다는 얘기예요. 안에서 일어나는 일은 안에서 할 수 있게 돼 있는데 그건 모두 공심이 되어 움직이기 때문입니다. 둘 아니게 대처하거든요. 단순히 내쫓는 게 아니에요.

respond with your brain and body to take care of it. If you can go forward like this, putting one foot after another, responding to what's in front of you, then even though something is difficult, you can take care of what needs doing without getting too caught up in it.

Wouldn't it be great if everything that's going on in the world was visible to your eyes? But that's not the case. You can't see a virus entering your body, nor can you see what responses work against it. So what you need to know is that all minds are inherently connected as one, and how you can encourage them to work together as one. Then, what happens inside, unseen, can be taken care of because everything will be working together as one. Just trying to kick something out isn't really a solution.

그래서 이 마음법이라는 게 그렇게 아주 기묘하고 광대무변하단 얘기죠. 여러분들의 마음이 이렇게 움직였는데 그게 그대로 성립이 됐다면 여러분들은 그걸 어떻게 생각하십니까? 때때로 가만히 보면 많은 분들이 마음으로 지어 놓고 이거 안된다고 팔팔팔팔 뛰는 거예요. 긁어서 부스럼을 만들어 놓고 힘들다고 그러거든요.

이 몸뚱이는 넉넉하게 그냥 자기 가는 대로 가게 내버려두고 그 주인공하고만 하세요. 이 몸뚱이를 가지고 아무리 용을 써 봐야 병만 나고 쓰러지게 되지 소용이 없어요.

That's why this practice of relying upon your fundamental mind is so unfathomable and so incredible. Imagine being able to give rise to a thought and have things work out. Well, you can do this. But sometimes people give rise to intentions that are just reflections of their own fixed ideas, and so when things don't go well, they make a fuss and complain that this practice of relying upon their fundamental mind doesn't work. It's like they keep swallowing broken glass, and then complain that their stomach hurts.

There's plenty of times when you should give your body a break and just place your focus on entrusting everything to your foundation, Juingong, and letting it take care of what's going on. If you don't entrust these things, and just run around trying to make things happen using your body and intellect alone, you won't accomplish much more than wearing yourself out.

이 주인공을 하나 붙들면 몸속에 있는 생명들을 다 붙잡을 수가 있죠. 또 주인공을 믿고 나가다 보면 급할 때는 하다못해 저 노간주나무라든가 향나무 같은 것도 응해줘요. 그 나무에 이파리가 얼마나 많습니까? 향나무 한 그루만 가져도 이파리 숫자가 얼마나 많아요? 만약에 그 이파리 숫자만큼이라도 나무에 있는 생명들이 한데 합쳐준다면 무슨 일을 못하겠습니까?

예전에 내가 아주 어렸을 때 우리 어머니가 박씨부인전을 보시고는 "얘! 박 부인은 이 세상에 아주 못나디 못나게 태어나서 어떤 집에 시집을 갔는데 남편이 장군이 되어 전쟁에 나갔단다. 그런데 적들에게 포위되고 말았지. 적들은 그 기세를 몰아 마을까지 쳐들어온다는데 너라면 어떻게 하겠니?"라고 묻는 거예요.

When you're centered on your fundamental mind, your Juingong, then it's like you're also holding all the lives in your body in the palm of your hand, so you can do something to help them out. If you entrust everything to your Juingong, and go forward, then in an emergency, even a juniper tree in your yard will respond to you. Imagine what happens when all the lives in that tree and all its needles work as one with you? What couldn't you accomplish?

When I was very young, my mother told me the story of Lady Park. She was born looking quite unattractive, but her family arranged for her to be married to a man from a good family, who eventually became a general. They were living near the northern border when war broke out. The war wasn't going well, and her husband's forces were being pushed back towards the army post they lived at.

앞뒤를 끊고 박씨부인전 얘기를 간단히 하자면, 박 부인은 과거에 천인㤾사이었는데 잘못을 저질러 혹이 이곳저곳에 나 있는 흉측한 얼굴을 갖고 태어나게 됐어요. 하지만 그렇게 태어났어도 굴하지 않고 공부를 많이 해 지혜롭고 기량이 출중했지요.

그래서 남편이 위기에 처했을 때 남복을 하고 달려가 포위된 남편을 구해줬죠. 그리곤 남편한테 안 들키려고 부리나케 말을 달려 집에 왔지만 뒤쫓아온 남편에게 잡혀 들통이 났어요.

그전까지만 해도 부인이 못생겼다고 방에는 들어가지도 않았는데 자기를 구해준 사람이 바로 자기가 홀대하던 부인이라는 사실을 알고 부인을 다시 보게 됐죠. 그 남편도 원래 마음 폭이 넓어 어느 정도 사람 볼 줄은 알았는지 "당신은 그냥 보통 여느 사람이 아니야. 그래서 일부러 미웁게 보이게 했지?" 하면서 그날부터 안방엘 들어갔어요. 그 후 박 부인은 진정한 사랑을 얻으면서 우스꽝스럽고 못생겼던 얼굴이 아주 맑고 뽀얗게 다시 탄생을 했지요.

To give some background, Lady Park had been a heavenly being in her past life, but due to past mistakes, she was reborn with an ugly face and had bumps all over her skin. However, she didn't give up and practiced diligently, and so became wise and outstanding in her abilities.

So, when her husband was in danger, she disguised herself with men's clothing and went to help. She managed to save him, but left quickly to avoid him recognizing her. Nonetheless, he'd seen her and what she did.

Their marriage had been arranged by their parents, with no regard for his wishes, and he hadn't been attracted to her anyway. So, he'd treated her indifferently, and had never once entered her bedroom. But after he'd seen her fighting with so much courage and skill, he began to consider her other qualities. "She really is quite extraordinary. I wonder if she chose to

그렇게 평화롭게 지내던 와중에 방심을 틈타 적군이 갑자기 쳐들어오는데 속수무책으로 당하다 보니 할 수 없이 초당울타리로 심어 놨던 향나무와 노간주나무의 이파리들을 전부 군사로 보이게끔 박 부인이 도술을 쓴 거예요. 그래서 적군이 보기에 이쪽에 군사가 엄청 많아 보이니까 마을까지 쳐들어오지 못하고 그냥 후퇴를 했지요. 여러분들은 이 이야기가 황당한 것이라고 생각할 수도 있지만 이게 부처님법에서는 그렇지가 않아요. 지금도 벌어질 수 있는 일입니다.

be reborn with an ugly appearance so she could move through the world without being harassed or made into a trophy?" He began to regard her with true affection, and, oddly enough, her once ugly complexion turned clear and bright.

Later, when the land was at peace, the enemy suddenly attacked, and caught the army off guard. They were helplessly beaten. As the enemy advanced upon the army outpost where Lady Park and her husband lived, she used a spiritual ability to make the needles of the juniper hedge around her home appear to each be a soldier. For although the outpost had strong walls, it didn't have enough soldiers to fight off an army. Thus, to the enemy, the outpost ended up looking like it was full of soldiers, so they retreated without attacking. You might think this story is ridiculous, but this is possible for someone who had realized the depths of the Buddha's teachings. Even today, this is possible.

사람이라 하면 고등동물이기 때문에 여러분은 부처가 될 수 있는 자격을 99% 갖췄어요. 이 말이 뭔 줄 아세요? 마음 하나만 까딱 잘하면은 100%가 된다는 얘기죠. 그런데 하등동물로 수없이 살아오던 그 습[13]이 남아 있기 때문에 그 습에 의해서 자기 마음을 자기가 마음대로 못하는 게 탈인 겁니다.

사람으로 태어나기까지 그 어려운 고비를 수억 겁 년 동안 다 넘기고 이제 1% 남은 건데 그 한 발짝 박차고 내걷는 게 많은 분들한테 그렇게 어려운가 봐요. 사실 자기 마음을 가지고 왜 자기 마음대로 못하나, 죽든지 살든지 그까짓 거 내팽개치고 하는 건데 왜 자기 마음을 자기 마음대로 못하나 하는 생각이 들 때가 있어요.

---

13. 습(習): 현재뿐만 아니라 과거 수억 겁 년 동안 행하였던 모든 행위들(말, 행동, 생각 등)이 버릇이 되어 잠재여력으로 남아 있는 것을 말함.

Human beings are such high-level animals that all of you are already 99% of the way to becoming a buddha. You have all of the potential needed to become a buddha. This means that if you can just use your mind wisely and put that into practice, that's all you need to reach 100%. However, because of the deeply ingrained habits you've developed over countless lives as a lower animal, you get caught up in using your mind in unwise ways.

We've gone through eons of hardship in order to be born as a human being, and now, taking that last step forward seems so hard for people. It's frustrating for me to see this. Whatever is coming to you, even life and death, you don't have to worry about it. Just input it into your foundation and go forward. So why aren't people doing this and using their minds to take this last step?

우리가 처음 여기 안양에 왔을 때가 겨울철이라 김장할 시기였는데 큰 다라나 항아리 같은 것들이 하나도 없었거든요. 신도들도 없었고 아무것도 없었죠. 돈이 없어 창틀이며 문짝이고 할 것 없이 달다 만 것도 있었고 페인트칠도 하다 말고 공사가 끝났으니 항아리 같은 거 살 돈이 어디 있었겠어요?

그래서 내가 나한테 얘기했습니다. '야! 김장은 해야 한겨울 날 텐데 다라도 없고 항아리도 없고 큰 그릇들이 없잖아, 그러니 네가 좀 알아서 해!'라고요. 이러고 그냥 잊어버렸어요. 배추는 구해다 쌓아 놓고 그런 지경이 되었으면 많은 사람들이 아등바등했을 테지만 나는 김장을 못 하든 하든 크게 상관하지 않았어요. 김치를 하게 되면 하고 못 하게 되면 못 하는 거지, 안 그래요?

When I first came to Anyang, winter was just beginning, and it was the time for making kimchi. However, I didn't have any of the big, clay jars used to store kimchi. And at that time, there were no members nearby to ask for help. I'd just finished the original building here at the Seon Center, and had the roof and outer windows and doors installed, but the inside was only about a third finished, and there was no money left at all. I had cabbages, but there was nothing left to buy anything else. Without that kimchi, there would have been almost no vegetables until spring, not to mention the protein it provided.

So, I said to myself, "I need to make kimchi for a long winter, and we need jars, mixing bowls, and spices. So, you take care of it!" and didn't think about it again. If all you had was a pile of cabbages and were in a similar situation, a lot of people would have been really stressed, but I

그런데 그날 밤 저녁에 청량리에 사시는 '이소저'라는 할머니가 별안간 여길 오고 싶더라는 거죠. 김장 때도 되었는데 그릇도 없을 것 같아 큰 다라 다섯 개 사고 그 집에 있는 큰 항아리 다섯 개와 쌀 두 가마니를 트럭에 싣고 밤중에 왔길래 내가 그랬어요. '허 참! 있긴 있구만.' (대중 웃음) 허허허.

또 얼마 전에는, 울산에서 불사를 하는데 돈이 하나도 없다는 거예요. 그런데 신도들은 돈이 있는지 없는지, 또 돈이 없으면 어떻게 해야 할지 다들 아무 생각이 없으니 스님들 걱정이 이만저만이 아니었지요.

didn't really care whether I could make kimchi or not. If I could make kimchi, I'd make it, and if I couldn't, then I wouldn't. Right?

But late that day, a follower who lived on the far side of Seoul in Cheongnyangni, Mrs. Lee So Jeo, suddenly wanted to visit me. She knew it was the kimchi season, and didn't think there would be any supplies here, so she hired a truck and loaded it up with five huge clay jars, five big mixing bowls, spices, salt, and two 80 kilogram bags of rice. When she showed up in the middle of the night, I had to laugh to myself about the ability of this connection we all share.

Not too long ago, the *sunims*[10] at the Ulsan branch said they wanted to build a traditional temple and move out of the rented office space they were using, but that they didn't have

---

10. Sunim / Kun Sunim: Sunim is the respectful title of address for a Buddhist monk or nun in Korea, and Kun Sunim is the title given to outstanding nuns or monks.

그래서 찾아온 그 스님한테 말했어요. "네가 있다면 할 거고, 없다면 못할 거니까 안달하지 말아라. 1년이 간들 어떻고 10년이 간들 어떻고 100년이 간들 어떠냐, 꼭 지으라고 너한테 꼬리표 붙여 놓은 것도 아닌데. 부처님이 계시다면 할 거고, 안 계시다면 못 할 거 아니냐. 그게 바로 네 자성불이다, 이거야. 자성불이 있어야 통하는 거지, 자성불이 없으면 통하지 않는다는 얘기지. 그러니 네가 알아서 해라"라고 그랬죠.

enough money. What's more, they were worried that the temple members wouldn't be able to support such a temple or its construction.

So I told them, "It depends upon you. If you have faith in your true self, Juingong, and thoroughly entrust this to it, then it will take care of things. If you don't, then it won't. So don't get caught up in chasing all kinds of concerns about it.

"What does it matter if it takes one year or ten years, or even a hundred years to finish the temple? No one put a tag on you saying that you have to build a temple. Where did that need to build a temple come from? It came from deep within you, from this inner buddha that connects all things. So rely upon this inner buddha! Then everything will communicate through it and work together as one whole."

여기 스님들이 돈을 쌓아 두고 남을 도와주고 그러는 게 아니에요. 우린 털털이로 살아요. 털털이로! 털털이 아세요? 허허허. (대중 웃음) 사람이 털털이로 살면 아무것도 걱정이 없어요. 누가 훔쳐갈까 봐 걱정도 없을 거고요. 신도님들이 가져오는 거 감추는 마음도 없어야 해요.

옛날에 어느 중이 그렇게 감추는 마음이 있었는데 죽어서 큰 구렁이가 됐더래요. 그리고 비늘 속에 구더기들이 잔뜩 붙어 살았는데 그 구더기들은 다름이 아니라 바로 그 중한테 시주한 사람들이었어요. 줬던 대가를 내놓으라고 구더기들이 웅성거리니 그 놈의 몸뚱이가 살 수가 있어야 말이죠.

절은 망했는데 구렁이만 남아서 자기를 구해줄 도통한 스님을 만나려고 수년을 기다렸어요. 그러던 어느 날 기다리던 스님이 턱 오셨더라는 거죠. 그러니까 그냥 바지자락을 휘감고선 잡고 늘어진 거예요.

Our temple doesn't actually have a lot of money. The sunims here live with empty pockets. (Laughs.) If you don't have anything, you don't have to worry about someone stealing it. Furthermore, no sunim should obsess over what the lay members donate.

A long time ago, there was a monk who hid away money that had been donated by lay members. But after he died, he was reborn as a large snake. There were a lot of maggots living in the scales of that snake, but those were part of the mind of donors who had expected something in return. They were always nipping at him, demanding to be rewarded, so his existence as a snake was extremely unpleasant.

The temple gradually fell into disrepair, but the snake still remained, waiting for years. It was waiting for someone awakened who could help him. Finally, such a person came, in the

일반 사람들 눈에는 스님 발목을 휘감은 구렁이만 보이겠지만 스님은 그게 누군지 아는 거죠. 구렁이가 사정사정하면서 매달리니 스님이 그냥 지나칠 수가 없었어요.

그래서 구렁이가 하는 이야기를 다 듣고는 우두커니 서서 보다가 "정히 그렇다면 알겠노라"고 하자 옆에 있던 사람은 스님이 허공에 대고 헛소리하는 것처럼 보이니까 "저 스님 정신 나갔군! 정신 나갔어!" 이러거든요. 그래도 스님은 그런 소리들은 듣는 둥 마는 둥 하고 다음 날 구렁이를 천도[14]해 줬어요.

---

14. 천도(薦度): 사후에 영혼이 가야 할 길을 자신의 차원대로 제대로 갈 수 있도록 인도하여 주는 것. 일반적으로 불교의식으로 행해지는 천도재는 주로 독경, 시식, 불공 등을 베풀어 망자의 길을 인도하여 줌.

form of an awakened sunim. The snake wrapped itself around his leg, and refused to let go. Other people just saw a snake acting bizarrely, but the sunim looked inward and understood who the snake was and what it wanted. With the snake begging for help so desperately, he couldn't just walk away.

He listened to everything the snake said, and then said, "Okay, if that's your situation, I'd better help." To anyone nearby, the sunim must have seemed like a crazy person, talking to a snake. But other people saying things like that was irrelevant to him. The next day he even had a *cheondo*[11] ceremony to help the snake move forward.

---

11. Cheondo: This involves helping the consciousness of the dead to move forward on their own path. It can happen that beings become stuck in their fears, attachments, and illusions, etc., and so can't move forward. Cheondo often involves a special ceremony, but not necessarily, which in a sense educates the consciousness, and so allows it to move forward at a level that more accurately reflects the level they achieved while alive.

그러니까 구렁이가 "스님, 스님! 내 껍데기가 벗겨지걸랑 그것 좀 태워 주십시오. 스님이 태워 주셔야 내가 다시는 구렁이로 태어나는 일이 없을 것 같아요" 그러더래요. 그래서 스님께서 구렁이가 원하는 대로 태워 주고 난 후, 구렁이가 말한 데를 가 보니까 엽전을 감춰 놨던 항아리가 몇 개나 있더래요. 그 돈으로 동네 어려운 사람들을 다 도와주고 법당을 잘 지어서 딴 스님이 와서 살게 하고 그 스님은 거기를 떠났대요.

이 세상에는 여러분들이 믿기 힘든 소소한 이야기들이 참 많지만 이런 이야기들을 거짓이라고 생각하지 마세요. 혼자 방에 앉아 있다 보면 어떤 때는 왔다 갔다 하는 노인네들도 있고 또 **예수재**[15] 지내 달라고 하는 먼저 간 자손들도 있는데 마음으로 그 부모들을 잘 보내고 나면 꼭 그 대(代)의 조상이 와요. 참 고맙다고요. 아프지 않고 잘 가게 된 거죠.

---

15. **예수재(豫修齋)**: 살아 생전에 공덕을 닦아 사후 혹은 다음 생에 받을 과보의 고통에 떨어지지 않기 위해 미리 지내는 의식.

The snake had asked the sunim to please cremate its body, saying that if its snake form was completely burned up, then it would escape from being born as a snake again. After the cheondo ceremony, they found that the snake had already died, so he had its body cremated as it had wanted.

Then he went to where the snake said it had hidden the lay members' donations. There, he found several buried clay pots filled with old coins. He took that money and used it to help the needy in the area. He stayed for a while longer, helping to rebuild the temple and found a sunim to stay there and perform the daily ceremonies. After that was taken care of, he left and continued on his way.

There are a lot of stories like this that you may have a hard time believing, but don't automatically dismiss them. When I sit alone

지극한 마음의 공덕

여러분들이 오늘 한 푼 두 푼 모아서 여기 이렇게 올린 것이 정말 누가 한 것보다 더 고마웠어요. 청년분들이 올린 거요. 그래서 가져오신 거를 일체제불과 더불어 모두에게 알려야겠다 생각했습니다. 일체제불의 마음이 바로 보살이니까요. 그렇게 알려 놓으면 어떻게 되는 줄 아세요?

예를 들어, 청와대 들어가고 싶다고 해서 누구나 들어갈 수 있는 거 아니잖아요. 그런 것처럼 우리가 죽으면 서**천국** 西天國[16]에 들어가야 할 텐데 청와대처럼 아무나 들여보내질 않아요.

---

16. 서천국(西天國): 아미타불의 정토(淨土). 모두 한마음이 되어 아무것도 내놓을 것이 없는 한자리를 일컬음.

생활 속 참선수행 시리즈(18) 마음을 편안하게 두고(휴헐할휴)

잘하고 있어

편안해져도 괜찮아

in my room, sometimes I encounter spirits of the elderly coming to visit, as well as the spirits of adult children asking me to help ease the passing of their still living parents. After helping them move on, ancestors from their family line will sometimes come to me and express their gratitude, for now those people are no longer suffering and have been able to move forward on their own path.

The karmic affinity of a sincere heart

The offering you all made today is so precious. To see so many sincere young people offering what little you have was so touching that I took that and shared it with this one mind of all buddhas, which manifests as nondual compassion and love. When such sincere hearts combine with this one mind, you can't even guess what might happen.

여러분들이 어떻게 살아왔는지 다 훑어보고 법원장, 검사, 판사 같은 일을 하는 분들이 그 서류를 준비해서 올려야 그 사람이 어디로 가고 어떻게 태어날지 판단이 나는 거죠. 데려갈 때도 마찬가지입니다. 거기에 힘 좀 더 보태는 거예요. 비유해서 말하자면 그렇습니다.

제가 이런 얘기를 한 것은 오늘 우리의 선한 마음이 진짜로 일체제불의 마음과 하나가 되었기 때문이에요. 여러분들은 연등燃燈부처가 제각기 아마 이 다음에 다 모시고 갈 거예요. 물론 후에라도 마음을 나쁘게 쓴다면 그런 사람은 경찰한테 붙들려가는 것과 같은 일을 당하겠지만요.

Let me give you an example, even though someone wants to go visit *the Blue House*,[12] that doesn't mean they can actually just go there and enter. Likewise, when you die, then, for the sake of your development, you really should go to the Western Pure Land of Amitabha. But they don't let just anyone in. So, figuratively speaking, it's as if prosecutors and judges examine the record of how you've lived, and issue an order stating where you can go and what form you can be born with. Then they determine who you'll be greeted by at the moment of death, and what form your transport will take. So what I did was like putting a good recommendation in your file. I'm simplifying this a bit, of course!

I'm speaking of this to you because our good intentions and gratitude became one with the all-encompassing mind of buddhas. Perhaps in

---

12. The Blue House: The official residence of the president of the Republic of Korea

어찌 됐든 그렇지만 않다면 연등부처가 모시고 가는 연등을 타고 가는 거죠. 그러니 서천국에 들어갈 때, 청와대라고 합시다, 청와대 들어가는 데 그냥 무난하게 통과할 수 있어요. 이렇게 함께하신 분들에 대해 하나도 빼 놓지 않고 알렸어요. 그것은 **한생각**[17]이면 되는 거니까요. 너무나 고마워서요. 뭘 줘서 고마운 게 아니라 그런 생각을 낸 게 고마워서요.

그러니 여러분들의 마음, 일체제불과 하나가 되었던 그 마음이 바로 공심으로서 **공덕**[18]을 짓게 되는 거고 공심으로서 공덕을 또 받는 거죠.

---

17. 한생각: 어떤 생각을 우리들 내면의 근본자리에 입력시키거나 맡겨 놓았을 때, 근본을 통해 나오는 생각은 우리들 몸속의 모든 생명들뿐만 아니라 이 세상의 만물만생에 전달되며, 일체가 그 생각에 응하게 됨. 보이지 않는 정신계, 즉 우리들 근본마음을 통해 일으켜지는 생각은 물질계에서 현실로 나타나게 됨. 이렇게 근본을 통해 나오게 되는 생각을 한생각이라 함.

18. 공덕(功德): 다른 사람이나 대상을 나와 둘로 보지 않고 '내가 했다'라는 생각을 하지 않으며 조건 없이 도와주는 상태, 혹은 그렇게 함으로써 나오는 결과를 뜻한다. '함이 없이 하는 것' 즉, '내가 이러이러한 일을 했다'라는 생각을 놓아버리고 해야 공덕이 됨. 아무런 조건 없이 하는 행(行)이라야만 만물만생에게 이익이 될 수 있음.

the future, the buddha known as "Light Giver" will come to greet each of you at the moment of death. Of course, if later in life you use your mind in a bad way, it could be some rough-looking cops who come to greet you. (Laughs.)

Anyway, the buddha "Light Giver" will greet you and take you on a shining lotus flower to the Western Pure Land. And then it will be like being admitted to the Blue House without any delay or hassle. I've informed all buddhas about every single one of you. All of this was done with a single thought through our foundation. I was so touched not because of the money, but because you'd had the intention to do something like this.

This mind of yours that became one with the minds of all buddhas gave rise to *virtue and merit*[13]

---

13. Virtue and merit: Here this term refers to the results of helping people or beings unconditionally and non-dually, without any thought of self or other. It becomes virtue and merit when you "do without doing," that is, doing something without the thought that "I did such and such." Because it is done unconditionally, all beings benefit from it.

이렇게 공심이 돼야 주는 것도 돼요. 공심이 되어 주고받고 가는 사람들은 하다못해 저 길에 나 있는 풀잎 하나와도 서로 통합니다.

고통과 시련조차도
내 근본에서 온 것

여담을 좀 할게요. 옛날에 내가 이 공부를 하면서 이리저리 다닐 때, 산천초목과 마음으로 소통하며 인사를 나누는 것이 익숙지 않다 보니까, 사람들이 보기에 정신 나간 사람처럼 보였겠지요. 나무가 나한테 인사를 하면 융통성 있게 그냥 인사를 주고받았으면 되는데 그렇게 못하다 보니 미쳤다는 소리도 많이 들었어요. 거지 취급도 많이 받았고요. 경찰서에 끌려간 적도 있는데 거기서 도민증이나 시민증 보여 달라고 해도 그런 게 내가 어디 있어야 말이죠. 없다니까 더 들볶였죠.

through this combined functioning as one mind, and, as one, you'll receive that virtue and merit. Only when you become one with others like this, will you be truly capable of giving. Someone who can both give and receive like this can also communicate with everything, even a lonely blade of grass beside the road.

Seeing even suffering and hardships as something from my foundation

Let me digress for a bit. Way back when I was wandering around the mountains and just practicing relying upon my fundamental mind, I would be greeted by the mountains and streams and trees. I would return their greetings, bowing and speaking with them as I would with any other person, so, to other people, I must have seemed like a crazy woman. When the trees greeted me, I could have responded to them through mind,

그리고 어린애들이 더 무섭더라고요. 한번은 이런 일이 있었어요. 애들이 여럿이서 놀이를 하는데 참외를 흐르는 물에 띄워 놓고 그거를 누가 먼저 잡나 경주를 한 거죠. 그런데 나는 그것도 모르고 목이 마르니까 그 냇물에서 물을 먹고 있다가 참외 하나가 흘러내려오니까 그걸 아무 생각없이 집은 거예요. 그게 다 공부였던 거지요. 집는 순간에 그 애들이 뛰어와서는 저 미친 거지가 우리 참외를 훔쳤다고 하여 경찰서까지 끌려갔어요.

벌을 주려면 나에 대해 뭐가 있어야 되니까 사흘 나흘 걸려 우리 집에 연락하고 내 신원조회를 했지요. 그러는 동안 나는 풀이 나 있는 맨바닥에 벽과 지붕만 해 놓은 방 같은 데에 갇혀 있었어요. 별게 없으니까 나중에는 그냥 가라고 그러더군요. 그래서 그때 많은 공부를 했지요.

but I wasn't used to doing that, so I got called crazy a lot.

I was often treated like a beggar, and the police arrested me a bunch of times, taking me to whatever place they were using as a police station and harassing me. I didn't have an identity card, so they were particularly unpleasant.

Another time, there was a bunch of kids playing in a stream, where they would float a small yellow melon in the water and then race downstream to see who could catch it. I was thirsty and was getting a drink from the stream when the melon floated by me. I just picked it up and set it aside without thinking. As soon as I did that, the kids started screaming that a crazy beggar had stolen their melon.

The police came and hauled me to the old farmhouse they were using as a police station. They were trying to charge me with theft, and

나중에 또 빨치산으로 오해받아 붙들려서 고문을 당했을 때도 그 사람들을 나무라지 않았어요. 왜냐하면 내 자불自佛이 나를 단련시키고 공부시키기 위해서 한 거라는 걸 아는데 내가 누구를 원망하겠어요. 오히려 감사하지. 그때 다친 거는 얼마 안 지나서 나았어요. 위로의 말이었겠지만 누가 그러길 죄 없이 맞은 매는 금방 낫는다고 했는데 그 말이 생각나더군요.

재미있는 일이 또 하나 생각났어요. 예전에 사복형사들이 뭣 때문인지 나를 어느 시골집 방에다 며칠 가둔 적이 있었는데 거기서 이유도 모른 채 맞았죠.

spent three or four days trying to contact my family to verify my identity. In the meantime, they kept me locked in an old storeroom with a dirt floor. In the end, they had to let me go because I hadn't actually done anything. That experience gave me a lot to practice with.

Later, I was even mistaken for a communist guerrilla and tortured. I knew that it was the buddha within me, working to train and teach me, so I didn't blame them. Instead, I just tried to use that as practice. Further, the injuries I suffered healed very quickly, and made me remember an old saying, that a wound from an undeserved injury heals right away.

Sometimes, things like this had a funny ending, too. One time, a detective locked me up for several days, without telling me why. The police would just hit me and yell at me without explanation. Here, too, it was just an old house they were using as a police station.

한참 있으니까 아무 소리가 없더라구요. 그런데 내 속에서 '얘, 문 좀 들어 올려 보자' 이래요. 그래서 방문을 살짝 들어 올리니까 끼워졌던 돌쩌귀가 빠지면서 문이 한쪽으로 젖혀지는 거예요.

젖혀지길래 나와 보니 책상이 양쪽에 있고 형사들이 모두 엎드려 자고 있더라구요. 건빵을 먹다가 잠이 든 건지 건빵 봉지들이 옆에 있어서 그걸 봉지째 챙겨 가지고 나왔지요. (대중 웃음)

그게 부처님 법이에요. 몽땅 어떻게 그렇게 자요? 소리도 많이 났는데. 내가 나와야겠으니 내 자불自佛과 그들의 자불自佛이 연결되어 같이 돌아간 거지요.

I was being kept locked in a room, when I realized that it had been a while since I heard any sounds from the outer office. Then, my true nature told me, "Hey, let's try to lift the door a bit." So, I lifted up on the door, and when I did, the hinge pins lifted out with it and that side of the door fell open enough for me to squeeze through. Then I just walked out into the room the police used for their office.

All of the police were still there, sitting in desks on both sides of the room – with their heads down on the desks, asleep! There was an open bag of those thumb-sized army biscuits sitting on one desk, so I took it with me as I walked out past all those sleeping policemen. (Laughs.)

Everything that happened was the manifestation of my inner buddha. Is it plausible that all of those policemen would fall asleep at the same time, or that they wouldn't hear the crash

그렇게 나가서 한 이틀 있으니까 상처가 아물고 나았어요.

또 어느 땐가 그 해에 눈이 많이 왔는데 어디 가서 잘 데도 없고 해서 소나무 위로 올라갔지요. 넓적하게 가지가 갈라진 데가 있어서 거기 앉았다 눈이 좀 녹으면 내려가야지 했는데 너무 고단해서 그만 잠이 들었어요. 그러다 잠이 든 채로 떨어져서 앞니 두 개가 부러졌죠. 그리고 그때 관리를 제대로 못 해서 고생을 많이 했어요.

결국엔 나중에 코 양옆으로 해서 볼따귀 아래까지 썩어 들어가 수술을 받았는데 그 수술이 뭐가 잘못됐다고 해가지고 다시 또 들어내는 바람에 얼굴이 이렇게 찌그러졌죠.

of the door falling open? This happened because the buddha within me connected to the buddha within them, and worked together. The injuries I'd received all healed within two days and left no aftereffects.

Once, when it snowed a lot, I couldn't find a good place to sleep, so I climbed up into the branches of a large pine tree. I rested there where it was dry, and planned to come down once the snow melted a bit. However, I was so exhausted that I fell asleep and fell off the branch, hitting my two front teeth on something as I fell to the ground. The roots of those teeth died, but there was nothing I could do about them back then, and eventually they caused me a lot of problems.

As a result of those teeth, years later I developed a bad infection that spread up to my nose and sinuses, but surgery was unsuccessful. And then I had to have another operation, which

그래도 그 의사들을 원망한 적이 없어요. 왜냐하면 이 모습이라는 거는 잘생길 수도 있고 못생길 수도 있는데 그게 다 일리가 있는 거거든요. 잘생겼으면 내가 이렇게 중노릇하고 있나요? (대중 웃음)

여기 저 스님들도 전부 못났으니까 중노릇하고 있는 거죠. 하하하. (대중 웃음) 약삭빠르고 똑똑하고 그러면 이 공부를 못해요. 듬직하면서도 못났으니까 이 공부를 하는 거죠. 이 공부를 하면 세세생생 자유권을 얻어요. 자유권을 말이에요.

그러니까 여러분들도 살면서 자식을 낳고 기르는 와중에 힘들고 어려운 일을 겪을 때라도 좌절하지 말고, '그것도 역시 내 공부이고 내 식구가 전부 스승이다' 이렇게 생각하면서 한 걸음 한 걸음 나아가세요.

damaged the nerves in my cheeks and changed my appearance. But I've never blamed the doctors. Why? Because it's not worth getting too caught up in looks.

Look at our sunims here, if they were conventionally beautiful or good-looking, could they have become sunims? (Laughs.) Likewise, if someone's very self-centered or always calculating the angles for their own benefit, do you think they could practice? Our sunims may seem unusual from a worldly perspective, but they are mature and trustworthy, and practice well. They work at relying upon their fundamental mind, and so will free themselves from the cycle of birth, death, and clinging. In so doing, they'll experience true freedom!

So, don't be frustrated when you're having a hard time taking care of your family. Instead, take one step at a time and keep moving forward,

상대적인 스승이 없다면 내가 일상생활 속에서 공부를 못해요. 저 나무 한 그루를 보고서도 공부할 수 있고 깨우칠 수도 있어요. 요만한 거 하나도 버릴 게 없고 모든 게 다 내 스승입니다. 천칠백 공안千七百公案이 전부 다요. 왜냐하면 만물만생은 근본을 통해 서로 다 연결되어 돌아가기 때문이에요.

thinking, "This is also part of my practice of relying upon my fundamental mind, and my family is my teacher!"

Think of everyone and everything you encounter in life as a teacher. If you view even a branch on a pine tree as your teacher, then even something like that can help you learn and awaken. There's nothing that can't be your teacher.

Every single thing! Even the tiniest thing is one of the 1,700 *hwadus*.[14] Every single thing is connected to every other through this foundation and all work together through it, so every single thing can help you learn and awaken.

---

14. Hwadu(話頭, C. – hua-tou, J. – koan): Traditionally, the key phrase of an episode from the life of an ancient master, which was used for awakening practitioners, and which could not be understood dualistically. This developed into a formal training system using several hundred of the traditional 1,700 koans. However, hwadus are originally deep questions that arise from within. Thus, all of your own questions about your life can be your true, living hwadus.

하나로 연결되어 돌아가는

그러니까 이 모든 것들과 따로 떨어져 움직이는 자기는 없어요. 그렇기 때문에 고정된 '나'도 없고 고정된 그 무엇도 없는 거예요. 뭘 하나 봐도 본 순간 그건 과거가 돼 버립니다. 듣는 것도 그렇고 내가 하는 모든 행동이 그러합니다. 내가 만나는 상대도 또한 그렇게 변해요. 내가 이 사람을 지금 봤는데 본 순간 내가 본 그 사람은 과거가 돼서 없고 내 앞엔 새 사람이 있는 거죠. 그런데 그렇다고 해서 내가 만난 사람이 다른 사람인가요?

듣는 것도 보는 것도 다 마찬가지예요. 한 발 떼면 한 발 없어지는 이치에서 이렇게 빠르게 바뀌면서 돌아가는데 어느 순간을 붙들고 '했다, 안 했다, 봤다, 안 봤다, 들었다, 안 들었다'를 따질 건가요? 그래서 부처님 법에서 '이 세상엔 화해서 나툼만이 있을 뿐이다'라고 하는 거예요.

Connected and communicating as one

Because everything is connected and communicating like this, there's also no separate "me" that exists apart from everything else. Nor is there anything that's fixed and unchanging. No matter what you see, the moment you see it, it becomes something of the past. This is the same for what you hear and what you do. It's the same when you meet someone – the moment you see them, that interaction becomes something in the past, and is gone. Now in this instant, there's another person in front of you, yet they are also not a different person.

The same thing is true for what we hear and see. Likewise, one footstep disappears the moment the next step is taken. It all changes so quickly. Which moment are you going to hold onto? Which would you argue about? In

그러니 화하고 나투는 그 흐름 속에 우리는 순간순간을 볼 뿐이고 들을 뿐이고 만났을 뿐이죠. 무엇을 했다 안 했다 말할 수 있는 게 없어요. 그냥 모두가 이렇게 공하게 돌아가는 거니까 아둥바둥 착을 두고 애를 쓰고 울고불고 하면서 살지 마세요.

예전에 어떤 사람이 와서 남편이 밖에서 여자를 하나 또 보고 다닌다고 그래요. 자식들이 있더라도 너무 속상하니까 이혼하겠다고 울고불고하더라고요.

which instant would you claim that you did something or didn't do something, that you saw something or didn't see something, that you heard something or didn't hear anything? This is why in the Buddha's teachings it's said that throughout all the world, there's only transformation and manifestation.

So we're only seeing one moment, only hearing one moment, only experiencing one moment in this flow of manifestation. Likewise, there's no separate entity that could say, "I did," or "I didn't do." Everything is flowing like this, manifesting and changing every instant, so don't stumble through life clinging to things and crying over them.

Several years ago, a woman came to me in tears, saying that her husband was, yet again, keeping a woman on the side. She was angry and saying that she was going to divorce him. But

그런데 제가 그분한테 이 공부하는 사람들에게 해주듯이 말해줄 수가 없었어요. '당신 남편이 이 세상 부인을 다 자기 부인이라고 하더라도 그렇게 할 수 없는 사람이 그러는 거니까 잘난 거지'라고 말이에요. 그 부인은 그렇게 생각하기 힘들 테니까요.

이런 말 하면 좀 안 됐지만 그래서 정말 받아들이지 못하는 사람들에게는 그런 얘기를 안 해요. 게다가 나 싫다고 하면 그냥 편안하게 순순히 놔주는 것도 좋은데 자식들도 있고 그러니까 모든 것을 침착하게 그냥 주인공한테 관하라고 그랬습니다. 그저 '당신만이 그렇지 않게 해줄 수 있다'라고 하면서 자기 근본, 주인공에다 모든 걸 맡기고 부드럽게 말해 주고 부드럽게 대해 주라고 일러줬어요.

they also had children together as well, so that wasn't an easy solution.

There wasn't much I could say that would immediately help, because she didn't know anything about entrusting and relying upon her fundamental mind. She would have felt more hurt and angry if I'd told her the truth, that he was just the kind of man who's likely to always have women in his life. I could also tell that, regardless of his behavior, it would still be better for her and her children to stay with him.

At times like this, when people just can't accept what I really want to say, all I can do is talk to them about the basics of spiritual practice. So, I told her to calmly entrust everything to her fundamental mind, along with the intention that, "Only you can keep him faithful," and then to work at speaking to him gently and behaving gently.

더더욱 그래야 때로는 딸 노릇도 하고 때로는 동생 노릇도 하고 때로는 어머니 노릇도 하고 때로는 아내 노릇도 하고 때로는 할머니 노릇도 하면서 사람 폭이 넓어지는 거죠. 그렇게 해 줘야 또 남편도 남편대로 때로는 아버지 노릇도 잘하고 때로는 할아버지 노릇도 잘하고 때로는 오빠 노릇도 잘하고 때로는 남편 노릇도 잘할 수 있는 그런 사람이 되겠죠.

우리가 어떻게 살아야 내 몸뚱이 통 안에서 벗어나고 또 이 지구라는 큰 통 안에서도 벗어날 수 있을까요? 이 통에서 벗어나지 못하면 바깥에서 굴릴 수가 없어요. 내 몸통에서 벗어나지 못하면 내 몸뚱이를 마음대로 자기가 굴릴 수 없는 거죠. 그러니까 우선 이 몸통 안에서 벗어나야 해요. 그러려면 지금의 나를 있게 한 내 근본마음, 주인공에 집중하여 거기에 일체를 놓고 가야 합니다.

그러다 보면 길이 보여요. '주인공, 당신만이, 너가 있다는 걸 증명할 수 있어' 또는 '있으면 이렇게 해 봐'라고 자문자답도 하면서 놓고 가다 보면 나오게 돼 있어요.

In general, this is how you have to respond. Not only does it help you perform your role as a daughter, a sister, a mother, a grandmother, and a wife, but in so doing, it teaches your husband and helps him fulfill his role as a father, a grandfather, a brother, and a husband. In this way, he can become a deeper and more considerate person.

For nearly all people, life is like living inside of a series of barrels. These barrels are made up of the habits that we've carried with us, because they helped us as we've evolved to this point. But if we want to be free to grow and evolve to the next level, what do we have to do? At this point, you have to focus on entrusting everything to your inherent foundation, Juingong.

If you keep going forward like this, a path will appear. Take a look at what you face and say to yourself, "Hey! Juingong! You need to

석가세존도 자기 자불自佛인 연등불이 수기를 준 거기 때문에 수기 받은 놈도 없고 준 놈도 없다, 이 소리입니다. 바로 자기 자불自佛이 연등불이에요.

여지껏 나만 얘기했네요. 미련하게 혼자 너무 오래 얘기했어요. 질문 있으신 분 계시면 하세요.

생명의 존귀함을 대하는
깊이 있는 자세

질문자 1(男): 스님, 저는 안양 본원 청년회에 다니고 있는 학생입니다. 지금 고려대 행정학과 박사 과정에 있는데 여기 3층 법당은 제가 1년 전에 결혼한 장소이기도 합니다.

come forward and take care of this. Get out here and prove that you exist." As you keep doing this and letting go, your fundamental mind responds, and a way forward becomes clear. When Shakyamuni received the prediction of his future Buddhahood, it was from his own inner buddha. There was no separate person giving it to him, and no separate person receiving it. The buddha, "Light Giver," was also his own inherent buddha.

I've been talking for a long time now, so go ahead and ask me any questions you have.

Karma, abortion, and guiding children forward

Questioner 1: Sunim, I'm a student in the young adults group at the Anyang Center. I'm currently in a doctoral program for public

저는 결혼한 뒤로 저의 집사람을 통해 마음 법에 대해서 공부하게 됐습니다. 그리고 요즘 바쁜 중에서도 살아가면서 이런 게 행복이 아닌가 하는 생각도 하게 됐습니다. 큰스님께 깊이 감사드립니다. 제가 이 자리를 빌어 스님께 여쭤보고 싶은 게 있습니다.

제가 지금 한 열흘 정도만 있으면 아기 아빠가 됩니다. 한편으로는 가슴 벅차기도 하고 또 아기하고 좋은 인연이 되도록 마음도 내고 있습니다. 그러면서 요즘 아기들에 대한 관심을 갖게 됐습니다.

요새는 의료 기술의 발달로 아기의 성별과 상태를 일찍 알 수 있다 보니 선호하는 성별의 아기가 아니라던가 기아畸兒 판별을 받은 경우, 지우는 사례들이 있습니다.

administration at Korea University. This Dharma hall is also where I was married one year ago. It was through my wife that I learned about this practice of relying upon my fundamental mind. Even though I'm quite busy these days, there's a lot of wonderful things in my life. I'm deeply grateful to you, and given this opportunity, I'd like to ask you a question.

I'm going to be a father in about ten days. It's scary and exciting at the same time, and I'm giving rise to positive intentions to have a good relationship with my child. So, anyway, I've been thinking a lot about children these days.

With the development of medical tests and imaging, there have been more cases of parents having an abortion because of the sex of the child or the possibility of birth defects. Also, in the case of young men and women, they get together easily, and if they get pregnant, they usually

또 젊은 청년들 같은 경우, 쉽게 사랑에 빠져 임신을 하면 보통 낙태를 택하기도 합니다. 제 생각에는 아기를 가진 것 자체가 큰 복이고 자기한테 큰 인연이라 아무 생각 말고 낳아야 되는데, 간혹 가다 사람들이 그렇게 하지 않는 것 같습니다. 이렇게 낙태된 태아는 어떻게 되는지요?

근본적으로 여쭙고자 하는 건 이런 우리들의 생명 경시 사상에 대한 것입니다. 우리들이 생명에 대해 어떠한 자세를 가져야 되는지요? 요즘 같은 경우 IMF 외환 위기 때문에 생활이 굉장히 어려워져서 그런지 부모들이 자식을 매질하고 어떤 때는 버리기도 한다는 이야기를 뉴스에서 보았습니다.

이런 사건들을 보면서 저 아이들이 고통 속에서 평생 너무 불행하게 살아가는 거 아닌가 하는 굉장히 안타까운 마음이 들었습니다. 세상에 나와 보지도 못하고 죽는 아이들도 그렇고 세상에 나왔어도 불행하게 살다 죽는 그런 아이들을 어떻게 구원해야 되는지 여쭙고 싶습니다.

choose abortion. What happens to the spirit of a fetus that's been aborted like this?

In my opinion, having a baby is a great blessing and a result of a deep karmic relationship. Parents should embrace the child unconditionally, but sometimes people don't seem to do that.

My basic question is about our disrespect for life. What kind of attitude should we have toward life? These days, due to the (1997) financial crisis, life has become very difficult and I see on the news that there are more cases of parents abusing their children or even abandoning them.

Hearing about these children, I feel so sad at how hard their lives will be, and how uncertain their futures seem. I'd also like to ask you how we can help the children who die before they even come out into the world, as well as those who have been born but live in such unfortunate circumstances.

큰스님: 내가 지난번에 진주에 가서 이런 얘기를 했어요. 이 집 짓는 거나 아이 낳는 거나 똑같다구요. 집 짓기 전에 해야 하는 것들이 있는 것처럼 아이를 가질 때도 마찬가지예요. 아이는 생기기 전에 미리 택해야 합니다. 내가 고른다는 뜻이 아니라 좋은 영가와 인연이 되도록 모든 걸 근본마음에 맡기면서 사는 노력을 해야 한다는 뜻입니다.

그래서 아기가 들어서면 그때 본격적으로 태교를 합니다. 이렇게 해서 낳아 기르는 아이들은 아이들이 갖고 나온 그대로 이쁘게 잘 크고 잘 살게 되죠. 그런데 생각도 없이 놀다가 어린애가 생기면 그것도 처치 무랭이로 생각하고 떼어 버린다는 말이에요. 그게 **업**[19]이 되는 거죠. 인과가 되고 살생이 되는 거예요.

---

19. 업(業): 몸과 입과 뜻으로 짓는 일체의 행위.

Kun Sunim: Having a baby is the same as building a house. Just like there are things you have to do before you start building a house, there are things you have to do before you have a baby. You need to make a choice before you have a baby. This doesn't mean that you are going to choose your baby, rather, it means that you need to work at entrusting and letting go of everything to your foundation. In this way, a more spiritually developed being will be drawn to you.

Once you become pregnant, you have to practice prenatal education in earnest. The children who are born and raised like this are going to grow up beautifully and live well, able to make full use of their potential.

However, there are even some people who don't bother with birth control, and just plan on getting an abortion if they get pregnant. With that kind of attitude, that act will end up becoming karma and killing.

어떤 사람이 산부인과를 하는데 병원에서 이런 수술로 마음고생을 많이 한다고 그러더라구요. 아기를 들어낸다고 하는 것은 어떻게 보면 당사자들보다 그 일을 직접 해야 되는 의사들이 정신적으로 더 고통스러울 수도 있어요. 더구나 인과나 업이 뭔지 대충이라도 아는 의사들은 더 힘들겠죠.

여러분들 중에는 이분처럼 자기 직업으로 인해 어쩔 수 없는 살생을 해야 하는 분들도 있을 거고 그냥 먹기 위해 물고기나 닭 같은 동물을 죽일 때도 있을 겁니다. 그럴 때 이 공부하는 사람들에게 할 수 있는 얘기는 하나예요. 자기 주인공에 맞닥뜨리는 일체, 보는 거, 듣는 거, 그러면서 느끼는 거, 일체를 맡기고 그리고 거기서 나오는 걸, 나오는 대로 다시 맡겨 놓으라는 겁니다. 그렇게 하면서 가다 보면 마음속에서 자기 근본, 주인공과 대담이 되고 그게 나를 가르쳐 주는 스승이 됩니다.

I heard from someone who runs an obstetrics and gynecology clinic that they have a hard time performing abortions. If someone has an abortion, it could be more distressing for the doctor than the patient. Furthermore, it would be harder for doctors who know a bit about karma and cause and effect.

I'm sure some of you, like those doctors, are forced to kill as part of your jobs. Others have to kill animals like fish and chickens just to eat. When that happens, the one thing I want you to know is this: Entrust everything you encounter – what you see, what you hear, and what you feel. And then take whatever comes back from that and entrust it again. When you do so, then over time, you'll develop the ability to communicate with your fundamental mind, your Juingong, and it will answer you and become your teacher.

더 나아가 다른 사람을 도와줄 수도 있어요. 나만 그렇게 할 수 있는 게 아닙니다. 내가 그 의사분 얘길 듣고 그 집 편안하게 도와줬듯이 여러분들도 그렇게 할 수 있어요. 그런데 이런 도리를 모르고 죽이게 되면 죽이는 일들이 악업이 되고 살생이 되는 거죠.

집안의 아픈 사람을 위해 잉어를 한 마리 잡아 고아 먹일 때라도 그 뼈와 살이 약이 되어 아픈 사람을 도와주는 데 큰 힘이 됨을 알고 감사의 마음으로 내 근본자리에 모두 놓으세요. 그래야 그 잉어와 내가 둘이 아니게 되어 나와 함께 같이 진화가 됩니다.

남의 생명을 내 생명같이 생각 안 하고 그냥 죽이면 그건 살생이에요. 그러니 이 도리를 모르고 태아를 낙태하면 부모나 의사나 전부 다 그게 업이 되어 돌아가 좋을 거라곤 하나도 없게 되는 겁니다.

If you keep going forward doing this, then you can help others like I do. I'm not the only one who can do this. You, too, can help the people you encounter, and help them and their families become at peace and more settled. However, if you don't know about entrusting everything to your fundamental mind, and you kill other lives, then that action becomes killing and harmful karma.

When someone in your family is ill and you go catch a carp to make soup for them, entrust that to your fundamental mind with your gratitude for the help and healing that will come from those bones and flesh. Then that carp can become one with you and is able to evolve with you.

However, if you aren't seeing other's lives as if they were your own, then your actions end up becoming killing. So, if you abort a fetus without knowing this spiritual practice of relying upon

그러니까 이 공부가 이상야릇한 공부죠. 하지만 이상하더라도 가짜로 생각하지는 마세요. 진짜입니다. 그런데 여러분들이 실천하고 경험하고 지혜를 넓히고 물리가 터져 봐야 진정으로 그 뜻을 알 수 있으니까, 현재의 나를 있게 한 수억 겁의 나, 즉 내 주인공을 꼭 발견해야 된다는 얘기입니다.

일단은 나를 있게 한 내 근본이 있음을 믿으세요. 믿고 모든 걸 거기다 맡기고 가다 보면 저절로 알게 돼요. 하다못해 머슴한테 일을 시킬 때라도 믿고 맡겨야 머슴이 신나서 일을 잘해요.

your fundamental mind, then that becomes heavy karma for the parents and the doctor. Yet, if you have tasted this practice, there's a path for you to mitigate the effects of your actions.

This practice has a lot of unexpected and mysterious aspects, doesn't it? But even though these may seem hard to believe, know that they're true, nonetheless. To understand these for yourself, you must broaden your wisdom and truly open your eyes. You absolutely need to discover the foundation, Juingong, that has created and guides this present "you." To do this, practice relying upon your fundamental mind and experiencing what happens.

For now, just have faith in this foundation that has enabled you to exist. Have faith in it, and as you work at entrusting everything to it, you will come to know it for yourself. It's like when you give a job to someone – you have to

그런데 믿지 못하고 의심하면 아예 일을 시킬 수도 없거니와 시켰다가도 발발발발거리며 '넌 믿을 수 없어' 하고는 일을 도로 뺏어 버리게 되니 아무것도 못 하는 거죠.

꿈에서 본 것도 놓고 가라

질문자 2(女): 스님! 저는 대전에서 왔습니다. 저는 제가 약간 영적인 사람이라고 생각을 합니다. 제가 스무 살 정도 될 때까지는 그냥 다른 사람하고 똑같았었는데요, 그때 집안도 어려웠고 저 자신도 너무나 힘든 일이 많았어요. 그래서 이 종교 저 종교 찾아다녔는데 그런 종교들이 다 기복적이었죠. 아마 바깥으로 찾아다녀서 그렇게 된 거 같아요.

어쨌든 제 안에 그런 싹이 있다 보니 제가 남보다 굉장히 직감이 있고 꿈을 잘 꾸는데 꿈이 맞을 때가 많았어요. 참고가 될 때도 있었지만 그런 남다른 직감을 갖는다는 게 저는 굉장히 힘이 들었습니다.

trust them with it and get out of the way. Then they'll probably do a good job with it, won't they? However, if you entrust your foundation with something but then begin to doubt it, it's like you keep trying to take away the job before it has a chance to finish.

Dealing with the things I see in my dreams

Questioner 2: Hello, Sunim! Somehow, I seem to have glimpses of the future. I was just like everyone else until I was about twenty, but around that time my family and I started going through a lot of hardships. I began going to a lot of different religious groups, but they all seemed to point outside of myself, and I think something about that accidentally gave rise to this ability.

Anyway, I seem to have ended up with a much more sensitive intuition than other people,

왜냐하면 어떤 나쁜 일이 있을 거라는 예감은 갖고 있는데 그걸 해결할 능력이 전혀 없다 보니 그게 절 더 앞서서 막 고통을 주는 거예요. 그런데 이 공부를 만나면서부터는 제가 많이 안정이 됐어요. 꿈도 많이 정돈이 됐구요.

예전에는 꿈을 너무 지저분하게 많이 꾸고 그래서 잠을 자도 잔 것 같지 않았었거든요. 그래도 여전히 지금도 꿈을 꾸고 있지만, 그게 도움이 될 때도 사실 많이 있어요. 예를 들면, 제가 어떤 사람한테 대행스님 이름을 전해 듣고는 92년 여름에 여길 처음 왔었는데 그 전에 스님이 여러 번 제 꿈에 나오셨었거든요. 얼굴도 뵙기 전인데 말이에요. 그런데 그때 큰스님을 한번 뵌 이후 여기 다시 오는데 1년 반이라는 세월이 걸렸어요.

and my dreams often give me glimpses of what really happens in the future. There were times when this was helpful, but overall it was very hard for me because even though I had a hunch something bad was going to happen, I was unable to do anything to stop it. I really began to suffer because I had to just wait and watch things happen. Thankfully, after I learned about this spiritual practice of relying upon my fundamental mind, I've felt a lot more at ease, and my dreams have begun to settle down.

In the past, I had such disjointed dreams that I couldn't sleep well. I still dream at night, but these days they are often helpful to me. For example, after I first heard about you, I saw you in my dreams several times.

The temple I'd been going to had emphasized praying to the Bodhisattva of Compassion, and I'd been doing that for about four years. Once, I

기복적으로 기도하며 다니는 것이 부처님 법이 아니라는 생각도 들고 회의감도 들었지만, 옛날에 다니던 절에서 관음기도를 3~4년 했고 절에 들어가서 스무하루씩 기도도 하고 그러다 보니 이런 걸 마음으로 정리하는 게 쉽지가 않아 94년이나 돼서야 다시 오게 됐습니다.

그때도 제가 여기 오게 된 마침표를 찍어준 계기가 있었는데, 꿈에 대행스님께서 나타나셔서 '내가 너한테 기회를 여러 번 줬는데 왜 이 마음공부를 안 하는 거냐?' 하면서 막 야단을 치시는 거예요. 여러 번 그렇게 스님의 꿈을 꾸었어요. 그래서 제가 여기 다시 오게 된 거죠.

그리고 제가 공부를 게을리할 때마다 스님이 꿈에 나타나셔서 저에게 숙제 거리를 주셨는데 한번은 허공에 줄 두 개를 딱 그으시더니 그 줄 두 개를 타고 앉으시고는 둥둥 떠서 말씀하시는 겁니다. "이게 무슨 뜻인지 네가 알아먹겠냐?"고요. 그런 숙제들이 제가 수행을 해나가는 데 도움이 많이 됐어요.

even prayed for twenty-one days straight while staying in the temple, so it wasn't easy for me to change my way of looking at things. I came here once in the summer of 1992, but then it took me another year and a half to come back. I finally left and came back here in 1994.

Around that time, you showed up in my dream and scolded me, "Even though I've given you so many opportunities, why aren't you working at learning to rely upon your fundamental mind?" I had several dreams like this. That's how I came back here again. Whenever I was lazy about spiritual practice, you appeared in my dreams and gave me some homework.

For example, in one dream you drew two lines in the sky, and then sat astride them and floated there.

문제는 그렇게 도움이 될 때가 많다 보니까 제가 꿈에 끄달리게 되는 거예요. 그래서 제가 어떤 일을 할 때 꿈에서 뭐가 나오면 제 마음대로 결정을 못 하는 거죠. 꿈에 나오는 거를 많이 참고하면서 살아왔기 때문이에요. 그러던 어느 날 가만히 생각을 해보니까 제가 꿈에 그렇게 끄달리는 거는 팔자 운명에 매여 사는 거와 같지 않나 하는 생각이 들었습니다.

큰스님: 참 나! 당신이 나를 못 보니까 당신 꿈에라도 나타나서 공부 거리를 준 건데 공부 거리나 받을 것이지, 왜 그 모습에 끄달리나요? 부처님의 모습은 개로도 됐다가 돼지로도 됐다가 소도 됐다가 말도 됐다가 나무도 됐다가 여자로 됐다가 남자로 됐다가 거지도 됐다가 이렇게 자꾸자꾸 바뀌는데 바뀔 때마다 그걸 붙잡고 늘어질 거예요?

You looked at me and asked, "Do you get it now?" These kinds of experiences really seemed to help my spiritual practice.

But because they helped me so much, I began clinging to whatever I was seeing in my dreams. When I needed to decide something, I felt a lot of pressure to go in the direction my dreams seemed to indicate. Then one day, I realized that clinging to my dreams was no different than deciding what to do based on my horoscope.

Kun Sunim: Don't cling to what you see. Even if you saw me in a dream and I gave you some homework, you're supposed to be doing the homework, not getting caught up in my appearance. Buddha can appear as a dog or a cow or a tree, as a beggar or a store clerk, as female or male. It keeps changing. Are you going to cling to every new shape?

질문자 2: 솔직히 말하면 그런 경향이 습관이 돼서 아직도 남아있어요.

큰스님: 그러니까 꿈을 꿔도 주인공에 그냥 놓고 가세요. 그리고 공부 거리라고 생각하는 그 꿈을 이해했으면 이해한 대로 '아, 그건 그런 거구나' 하고 놓고 가고, 또 이해가 안 가는 거는 '이해가 가게 하는 것도 주인공 너뿐이야' 하고 그냥 놔 버려요. 그러면 언젠가는 알아져요. 우리가 사는 것이 전부 지금 수시로 바뀌면서 가는데 그것을 다 붙잡을 거예요? 꿈을 붙잡는 것은 환상을 붙드는 건데 그게 얼마나 어리석어요? 용광로에 넣듯이 다 놔 버리세요.

질문자 2: 예. 알겠습니다. 감사합니다, 스님.

Questioner 2: To be honest, it became a habit that I still haven't overcome.

Kun Sunim: Take your dreams and entrust all of them. If you had one that taught you something about spiritual practice, then take what you learned and entrust that as well. If you didn't understand what was going on, entrust that, too, with the thought that, "My foundation will enable me to understand this." Then, one day, that meaning will become clear to you. Everything in our life is ceaselessly changing – is there any of it that you could hold onto? Getting caught up in worrying about your dreams is like worrying about a mirage. Pretty stupid, huh? Just dump it all into this furnace within you.

Questioner 2: Okay, I understand. Thank you, sunim.

큰스님: 신도들이 "스님, 꼭 오래오래 백 살까지 사세요" 그러잖아요? 우리 스님들도 그냥 내가 오래 살기를 바라고 그러는데 이런 것도 착이에요. 만약 누군가 날더러 '언제까지 살 겁니까?'라고 묻는다면 "사는 날까지 꼭 살게요!"라고 대답을 할 겁니다.

절대로 붙잡고 늘어지지 마세요. 전부 다 놓고 가다 보면 아주 편안해질 때가 옵니다. 그때 바로 믿음을 진짜 가질 수 있어요.

관세음보살[20]이다, 지장보살이다, 칠성이다, 주해신이다, 주산신이다, 지신이다, 이건 이름이에요.

---

20. **관세음보살**(觀世音菩薩): 세간의 괴로움으로부터 구원을 원하는 소리를 듣고 이에 응하여 고통으로부터 중생을 대자대비한 마음으로 구제하는 보살. 산스크리트로는 아바로키테슈바라(avalokitesvara)인데, 이는 곧 자재롭게 보는 이(觀自在), 자재로운 관찰이란 뜻으로써, 이 세상의 모든 것을 자재롭게 관조하여 보살핀다는 뜻.

Kun Sunim: People will sometimes say to me things like, "Sunim! Please live a long time, until you are at least a hundred!" But if someone asks me how long I will live, I always say, "I'll live for as long as I'm supposed to. You don't have to worry about that!"

Whatever you're experiencing, whatever you think you need, don't cling to it. If you keep letting go of everything to your fundamental mind, then there will be a time when you feel extremely calm and stable, and have a deep sense of faith in your fundamental mind.

As for *Avalokitesvara*,[15] *Ksitigarbha*,[16] the spirit of the Seven Stars, the spirit of the ocean, of the mountain, of the earth, of whatever – those are

---

15. Avalokitesvara Bodhisattva: The bodhisattva of compassion, who hears and responds to the cries of the world, and delivers unenlightened beings from suffering.

16. Ksitigarbha Bodhisattva: The guardian of the earth who is devoted to saving all beings from suffering and especially those beings lost in the hell realms.

용도에 따라서 딸이라 불렸다가 언니라 불렸다가 엄마라 불렸듯이 그 이름이 있어야만 되겠으니까 있는 거지 이건 다 부처님의 마음이에요.

그것만 그런가요? 내 마음도 부처님의 마음이에요. 내가 어떻게 마음 내느냐에 달려 있지요. 여러분이 '일체제불의 마음' 부르시죠? 그 노래에 있는 만큼만 하세요.

천년에 한 번 만나기 어려운
불법의 인연

질문자 3(男): 스님, 부산지원에서 왔습니다. 먼저 여러 **도반**[21]들과 스님들과 더불어 이 자리 함께하게 된 것이 너무나 감사합니다. 그리고 내가 곧 부처임을, 내 속에 자성이 있음을 끊임없이 일러주시는 스님, 감사합니다. 이 자리의 여러 도반들과 더불어 세세생생 물러서지 않고 정진할 것을 발원합니다.

---

21. 도반(道伴): 함께 도(道)를 닦는 벗.

all labels. It's like how you can be a daughter or a sister or a mother according to the circumstances.

In each case, there's a different name, but they all belong to the all-embracing essence of buddha. And to go one step further, your mind is also this all-embracing essence of buddha if you give rise to thoughts wisely. Do you remember the song I mentioned earlier, "The Mind of All Buddhas"? Just do that. Just put that into practice.

How can I get my family to come to the temple?

Questioner 3: Sunim, hello. I'm so grateful for your presence here today, as well as that of all of these fellow practitioners and sunims. Thank you for teaching me over and over that the essence of buddha is my essence, and is found within me. I vow to diligently work at putting this into practice, both in this life and in all my future lives.

큰스님: 당신 주인공, 불성佛性에 '네가 형성시켰으니 형성시킨 네가 울지 않게 해야지' 그렇게 하세요. '울지 않고 살게 해야잖아' 하고 말이에요.

그러니까 매사에 요만한 거 하나라도 걸리지 말고 근본마음에 다 놓으세요. 그러면 그것이 실천이 되고 공부가 되어 다시 한바다가 돼서 전부를 살릴 수 있어요.

Kun Sunim: Entrust your Juingong, your Buddha-nature, with the thought that, "Because you formed me, you should enable me to live without this suffering. You have to show me a way forward." Don't let yourself be hurt or shackled by anything.

So, let go of absolutely everything to your foundation. Then, all of those things you're encountering will become fuel for your practice, and will enable you to experience and understand this true nature of yours. And when they return to this one ocean, they will be transformed and come back out as something that can save all beings.

Questioner 3: When I see lay practitioners who come here with their families, I often envy them. My family claims to be interested in coming to the Seon Center, but they never quite

질문자 3: 스님, 제가 선원에 다니면서 가족들과 더불어 함께 공부하는 법우님들을 볼 때면 참, 부러울 때가 많습니다. 인연이 닿을 듯 닿을 듯 하면서도 인연이 닿지 않는 저의 부모 형제들을 볼 때면 정말 제 마음이 부족한 것인지, 때로는 불법佛法 인연이 따로 있는 것인지 그것이 궁금할 때가 많습니다. 스님께서 그에 대해서 한 말씀 해 주시면 고맙겠습니다.

큰스님: 이런 불법 인연은 천 년에 한 번 만나기 어렵다고 그랬습니다. 그런데 그런 마음이 얼른 와 닿겠어요? 그러니까 집이가 자꾸 기회를 만들어서 가족들이 함께 공부하게끔 해야죠. 편안하게 오게끔 자꾸 기회를 만들어 보세요.

질문자 3: 알겠습니다.

make it here. Sometimes I wonder if it's because my practice is lacking, or perhaps not everyone has the karmic affinity necessary to study the Buddha's teachings. I'd be grateful to hear your thoughts about this.

Kun Sunim: It's said that it is a rare and precious opportunity to come across these teachings about our inherent nature, and then learn how to rely upon it and apply it to our daily life. It's something that may only come along once in a thousand years. So how likely is it that they would just happen to have an interest in spiritual cultivation? What you need to do is keep creating opportunities for your family to learn this. Try to make stress-free opportunities for your family to come to the Seon Center.

Questioner 3: Okay!

큰스님: 가족들인데 집이가 다리를 놓지 않으면 누가 놓겠어요? 한생각만 잘하면 올 수가 있어요. 어떤 사람은 한생각을 잘해도 오지 않더라, 이러는데 그건 아직 마음의 응용이 자유자재로 되지 못하기 때문이에요.

영혼을 붙들고 해야 하는데 몸과 말로 몸뚱이를 끌려고 하니까 끌어지질 않죠. 그렇게 하면 요리 핑계 대고 저리 핑계 대면서 자꾸 달아날 걸요.

예를 들어, 자식들이나 형제들이 나가서 안 들어오거나 도둑질하거나 아주 나쁜 일을 하고 다녀도 그런 걸 스스로 안 하고 집에 들어오게 하려면 내 근본마음에 놓고 관해줘야 돼요. 그 사람한테 나쁜 말 하지 말고 나쁘게 행동하지 말고, 그 사람의 마음을 붙들어야 해요.

Kun Sunim: It's your family. If you don't become a bridge for them, who would? If you can thoroughly entrust your hopes to your foundation, then those can connect with them. But sometimes people come and say that despite their efforts at entrusting, their family still doesn't show any interest in spiritual practice. That's because they couldn't connect yet with their family's minds.

When your fundamental mind communicates with their fundamental mind and inspires them, they will come to the Center. But if you try to pull them here with words, they'll keep finding excuses to avoid coming.

In a similar way, even if your children or siblings stay out all night, or steal, or do something very bad, if you want them to change their behavior, you need to entrust that intention to your fundamental mind and observe. Don't

'둘이 아닌데, 네 주인공과 내 주인공이 둘이 아닌데, 너도 마음에서 잘 이끌어가야 할 자격이 있잖아' 하고 자꾸 이렇게 관하면 주인공, 그 근본마음이란 게 서로 연결되어 하나로 돌아가기 때문에 그 사람을 잘 이끌어 줄 수가 있게 돼요.

수차례 내가 이런 말을 하는 데도 그게 실천이 잘 안되나 봐요. 실천이 안 되면 배우자는 물론이거니와 피붙이인 자식조차도 이끌지 못해요. 마음으로 마음을 끌지 못하면 간단한 것도 어렵습니다. 마음이 스스로 오고 싶어서 와야지 마음이 싫은데 몸이 어떻게 와요?

give in to the desire for harsh words or actions. Instead, you have to connect with them on a deeper level.

Start by entrusting intentions like these, "Your foundation and my foundation are not separate. You have the ability to go forward in healthy directions, and are worthy of this." If you keep entrusting your intentions like this to your fundamental mind, then because your foundation and theirs are connected and work together as one, what you entrusted will help inspire and guide them.

I've told you this many times, but some of you don't seem to be putting this into practice. If you can't put it into practice, if you can't connect with their minds, you won't be able to help even your spouse or children, and it will be much more difficult to lead them forward to good paths. If they aren't feeling it in their heart, why would they voluntarily come here?

이 공부를 빨리 알게 하고 싶은 마음에 강제적으로라도 끌고 오고 싶겠지만 그런 건 소용없어요. 주인공은 둘이 아니니까 마음으로 부드럽게 인의(仁義)적으로 하세요. 잘 모르겠으면 스님네들한테 관하는 법 좀 가르쳐 달라고 하고요.

올 수 있는 사람이라면 빨리 끌어질 거고 그렇지 않다고 하더라도 그냥 마음으로 자꾸 이끌어 주세요. 그러다 보면 인연이 돼요. 아까도 얘기했지만, 이런 공부하는 데는 우리가 과거로부터 인연이 있기 때문에 만난 거예요. 과거로부터 인연이 없었으면 어떻게 이렇게 만나겠어요.

I'm sure you might want to bring them here because you want them to experience the benefits of this practice of relying upon our fundamental mind, but forcing them to come here is pointless. Your foundation is one with everything, so be generous and compassionate, entrusting everything to it. If you're unclear about how to do this, or are having problems with it, ask the sunims here to teach you.

If your family has a strong karmic affinity with this practice, they'll naturally be drawn to it. Even if they aren't, keep entrusting through your fundamental mind and, in so doing, that will become a karmic connection for them. We, as fellow practitioners, have met because of our connections from the past. How could we have met each other without some form of karmic affinity?

예전에 어떤 스님이 인연을 찾느라고 해만 뜨면 날마다 대낮에 등불을 켜 들고 파고다 공원을 그냥 헤매고 돌아다녔어요. 왜 낮에 불을 켜 가지고 다녔겠어요? 3년을 그렇게 했는데 묻는 사람이 하나도 없었어요.

그런데 어느 날 그걸 이상하게 생각한 한 청년이 스님께 물었어요. "스님은 왜 이렇게 대낮에 등불을 켜고 다니세요?" 그러자 스님이 사람 찾느라고 그런다고 하니 청년이 다시 물었죠. "대낮에 왜 불을 켜 가지고 사람을 찾아요?"

그러자 스님이 대답했어요. "바로 자네 같은 사람 말이야. 아, 이제야 찾았군." 이렇게 돼서 청년은 스님과 인연이 닿아 공부하여 크게 됐다는 얘기가 있어요.

Long ago, there was a monk who carried around a lit lantern in the daytime. He was searching for someone who had a deep karmic affinity with spiritual cultivation, and for three years, he wandered around a park that had once been the site of an ancient temple. He was always there with that lantern, but no one asked him about it.

Then one day, a young man saw this and thought it strange, so he said to the monk, "Why are you carrying a lantern in the daytime?" The monk answered that he was looking for someone. The young man asked again, "But why do you need a lantern in the daytime to look for someone?"

The monk answered, "To find someone like you. And look! I've finally found you!" This young man had a deep karmic connection with the monk, and went on to learn about spiritual cultivation, and became a great practitioner.

이 공부는 마음과 마음이 연결돼야 이끌어지는 거지 마음과 마음이 연결이 안 되면 상당히 그게 오래 가요.

어떤 종교를 믿든지 상을 걸어 놓고 거기다 "주여, 주여! 신이여, 신이여! 부처님, 부처님!" 하면 그것이 기복이거든요. 하나로 돌아가는 원리는 모르고 이름만 붙여서 불러대니 타의에서 찾는 거와 똑같은 거죠.

신이 들면 성령을 받았다고 하던가 뭐 그런 말들을 해요. 신이 들긴 든 거죠. 그런데 그건 자기 집을 자기가 사는 게 아니고 딴 게 들어와 사는 거예요. 말하자면 자기 집을 뺏기는 거고 자기 삶을 사는 게 아니죠. 때로는 미친 사람처럼 날뛰기도 해요.

This practice of relying upon our fundamental mind can guide others if there is a mind-to-mind connection like this, but when there isn't, guiding them can require quite a long time.

No matter what religion you believe in, if you raise up a statue and pray to it, saying, "Jesus!" "God!" "Buddha!" whatever, then you're seeing them as something that exists outside of yourself. You're thinking that you exist apart from everything else, and you're making it harder for yourself to realize that everything works together as one through our fundamental mind.

People go and act like this, and then if a ghost enters them, they say it's the Holy Spirit, or the hand of the gods, or something like that, but it's just a ghost living in their body. Now instead of you controlling your body, something else is in there, trying to use it as if they were the owner.

그러니 그게 얼마나 기가 막힌 일입니까? 수없이 과거로부터 진화해서 사람까지 됐는데 타의의 영가 때문에 내 집을 뺏기다니 그게 말이나 돼요? 두 눈 뜨고 멀쩡히 살아있는 내 몸을 뺏긴 건데, 분하지도 않습니까?

시간이 많이 지났네요. 우리 이제 그만 마칠까요? 여러 청년들이 바쁠 텐데도 진주지원에 가서 탑공원으로 가는 길을 만들어 줘서 참 고마웠어요.

그 길을 걸으면서 '아이구! 이런 진창에서 하나하나 블록을 놓느라고 정말 애를 썼겠구나!' 하는 생각을 했어요.

It's as if someone else has broken into your home, and is now trying to take over your life and boss you around. They may even cause you to act like a crazy person at times.

It's so stupid to fall victim to this! You've spent eons evolving to become a human being, but you'd lose all of that because of a ghost? It's like you're sitting there with your eyes wide open, watching, as your home is stolen. Wouldn't this make you furious?

I've been speaking for a while now, so let's stop here for today. I know you are all very busy, so thank you so much for coming down here to the Jinju branch and building the path to the stupa park.

As I was walking along that path, I thought to myself that you put in so much effort to set these paving stones one by one in the mud. I know you all aren't used to that kind of work, so to come

모두들 귀한 집 자식들일 텐데, 이 귀한 자식들이 자기 어머니 다니라고 길을 이렇게 해 놨으니 본인들 길도 트일 거예요. 참 좋네요. 이러고 잘 걸어 다니게 해놨으니, 여러분들에게도 참 좋을 거예요.

  감사해요, 정말.

down here and make this nice path to the stupa park for others to walk on is such a precious thing. And in so doing, you've opened up your own path. It really is wonderful. In working to build a path to make everyone's life a little better, you've also done something that's really good for you, too. Thank you so much.

한마음출판사 출간 도서
Books by Hanmaum Publications

뜻풀이 경전 (한영합본)

- 대행큰스님의 뜻으로 푼 금강경
  The Diamond Sutra: The Great Unfolding

- 만가지 꽃이 피고 만가지 열매 익어 (iF 디자인 어워드 수상)
  대행큰스님의 뜻으로 푼 천수경
  A Thousand Hands of Compassion

생활 속의 참선수행 시리즈 (한영합본)
Practice in Daily Life (Korean / English)

1. 죽어야 나를 보리라
   (To Discover Your True Self, "I" Must Die)
2. 함이 없이 하는 도리 (Walking Without a Trace)
3. 맡겨놓고 지켜봐라 (Let Go and Observe)
4. 마음은 보이지 않는 행복의 창고
   (Mind, Treasure House of Happiness)
5. 일체를 용광로에 넣어라 (The Furnace Within Yourself)
6. 온 우주를 살리는 마음의 불씨
   (The Spark that Can Save the Universe)
7. 한마음의 위력 (The Infinite Power of One Mind)
8. 일체를 움직이는 그 자리 (In The Heart of A Moment)

9. 한마음 한뜻이 되어 (One With the Universe)
10. 지구보존 (Protecting the Earth)
11. 진짜 통하게 되면 (Inherent Connections)
12. 잘 돼야 돼! (Finding A Way Forward)
13. 믿는 만큼 行한 만큼 (Faith In Action)
14. 병을 고치는 최고의 방법
    (The Healing Power of Our Inner Light)
15. 내 안에 의사가 있다구요?! (The Doctor Is In)
16. 마음: 최고의 연금술 (Turning Dirt into Gold)
17. 소용돌이 속에서 춤을 (Dancing on the Whirlwind)
18. 마음을 편안하게 두고 (Just Set It All Down)
19. 나를 알면 길이 보여요
    (Trust yourself and the path appears)

한글 단행본(Korean)

- 내 마음은 금부처 (상, 하권, CD 포함) 오디오북 및 e북
- 건널 강이 어디 있으랴 (도서 및 e북)
- 처음 시작하는 마음공부 1

영어(English)

- My Heart Is A Golden Buddha
- Like Lions Learning to Roar
- Standing Again
- Sharing The Same Heart
- Touching The Earth
- One Mind: Principles

스페인어(Spanish)

- El Camino Interior
- Vida De La Maestra Seon Daehaeng
- Enseñanzas De La Maestra Daehaeng
- Si Te Lo Propones, No Hay Imposibles

중국어(Chinese)

- 《我心是金佛》(간체자)
- 《人生不是苦海》(번체자, 개정판)

베트남어(Vietnamese)

- Không có sông nào để vượt qua (No River To Cross)
- Chạm mặt đất (Touching The Earth)

※위 책들은 오디오북, e북으로도 일부 제공됨

해외에서 출간된 한마음 도서
Other Books by Seon Master Daehaeng

English(영어)

- Wake Up And Laugh (Wisdom Publications)
- No River To Cross (Wisdom Publications)

German(독일어)

- Wie Fließendes Wasser
  (My Heart Is A Golden Buddha),
  Goldmann Arkana-Random House, Germany
- Wie Fließendes Wasser – audiobüch, SAGA/Egmont
- Vertraue Und Lass Alles Los (No River To Cross),
  Goldmann Arkana-Random House, Germany
- Wache Auf Und Lache (Wake Up And Laugh),
  Theseus, Germany
- Umarmt Von Mitgefühl
  (A Thousand Hands of Compassion),
  Theseus, Germany

Spanish(스페인어)

- Ningún Río Que Cruzar (No River To Cross),
  Kailas Editorial, S.L., Spain

Chinese(중국어)

- 《我心是金佛》(Traditional Chinese, Taiwan),
  橡樹林文化出版, Taiwan

Russian(러시아어)

- Дзэн И Просветление (No River To Cross), Amrita-Rus, Russia

Indonesian(인도네시아어)

- Sup Cacing Tanah (My Heart Is A Golden Buddha), PT Gramedia, Indonesia

Vietnamese(베트남어)

- Không có sông nào để vượt qua (No River To Cross), Vien Chieu, Vietnam
- Tỉnh thức và cười (Wake Up And Laugh), Vien Chieu, Vietnam
- Chạm mặt đất (Touching the Earth), Vien Chieu, Vietnam

Czech(체코어)

- Probuď se! (Wake Up And Laugh), Eugenika, Czech Republic

한마음선원 본원

경기도 안양시 만안구 경수대로 1282
(석수동, 한마음선원) (우)13908
Tel: (82-31) 470-3100 Fax: (82-31) 470-3116
홈페이지: https://www.hanmaum.org
이메일: jongmuso@hanmaum.org

국내지원

강릉지원 강원도 강릉시 하평5길 29(포남동), T.(033)651-3003
공주지원 공주시 사곡면 위안양골길 157-61, T.(041)852-9100
광명선원 충북 음성군 금왕읍 대금로 1402, T.(043)877-5000
광주지원 광주광역시 서구 운천로 204번길 23-1, T.(062)373-8801
대구지원 대구광역시 수성구 수성로 41길 76, T.(053)767-3100
목포지원 전남 목포시 백년대로 266번길 31-1(상동), T.(061)284-1771
문경지원 경북 문경시 산양면 봉서1길 10, T.(054)555-8871
부산지원 부산광역시 영도구 함지로 79번길 23-26, T.(051)4033-7077
울산지원 울산광역시 북구 달래골길 26-12(천곡동), T.(052)295-2335
제주지원 제주특별자치도 제주시 황사평6길 176-1, T.(064)727-3100
중부경남 경남 김해시 진영읍 하계로 35, T.(055)345-9900
진주지원 경남 진주시 미천면 오방로 528-40, T.(055)746-8163
청주지원 충북 청주시 청원구 교서로 109, T.(043)259-5599
통영지원 경남 통영시 광도면 조암길 45-230, T.(055)643-0643
포항지원 경북 포항시 북구 우창로 59(우현동), T.(054)232-3163

Anyang Headquarters of Hanmaum Seon Center
Tel: (82-31) 470-3175 / Fax: (82-31) 470-3209
onemind@hanmaum.org   www.hanmaum.org/eng

Overseas Branches of Hanmaum Seon Center

ARGENTINA
(Buenos Aires)
Tel: (54-11) 4921-9286 hanmaumbsas.org
(Tucumán)
Tel: (54-381) 408-2894 https://tuc.hanmaum.org

CANADA (Toronto)
Tel: (1-416) 750-7943 https://tor.hanmaum.org

GERMANY (Kaarst)
Tel: (49-2131) 969551
https://ger.hanmaum.org   hanmaum-zen.de

THAILAND (Bangkok)
Tel: (66) 61-413-7000 https://thi.hanmaum.org

USA
(Chicago)
Tel: (1-224) 632-0959 https://chi.hanmaum.org
(Los Angeles)
Tel: (1-323) 766-1316 https://la.hanmaum.org
(New York)
Tel: (1-718) 460-2019 / Fax: (1-718) 939-3974
https://nyk.hanmaum.org
(Washington D.C.)
Tel: (1-703) 560-5166 https://wah.hanmaum.org

책에 관한 문의나 주문을 하실 분들은
아래의 연락처로 문의해 주십시오.

한마음국제문화원/한마음출판사

경기도 안양시 만안구 경수대로 1282 (우)13908
전화: (82-31) 470-3175
팩스: (82-31) 470-3209
e-mail: onemind@hanmaum.org
hanmaumbooks.org

If you would like more information about these books or
would like to order copies of them,
please call or write to:
Hanmaum International Culture Institute
Hanmaum Publications
1282 Gyeongsu-daero, Manan-gu, Anyang-si,
Gyeonggi-do, 13908,
Republic of Korea
Tel: (82-31) 470-3175
Fax: (82-31) 470-3209
e-mail: onemind@hanmaum.org
hanmaumbooks.org